SEEING THE LIGHT

SEEING THE LIGHT

Evidence and Distractions of
Near-Death Experiences

MICHAEL J. ECKSTEIN
with John S. Knox
Foreword by Phil Wiley

WIPF & STOCK · Eugene, Oregon

SEEING THE LIGHT
Evidence and Distractions of Near-Death Experiences

Wipf & Stock
An Imprint of Wipf and Stock Publishers
199 W. 8th Ave., Suite 3
Eugene, OR 97401

www.wipfandstock.com

PAPERBACK ISBN: 978-1-6667-5323-3
HARDCOVER ISBN: 978-1-6667-5324-0
EBOOK ISBN: 978-1-6667-5325-7

03/08/23

For Rowan and Piper,
who never fail to show me how to be more like Jesus.

Contents

Foreword

FUNNY HOW LIFE WORKS.

On August 15, 2013, at 3:00 AM, Christ exploded into my life. I was three days into a solo, self-support, five-day odyssey, fast packing the John Muir trail from Happy Isles Yosemite to the Whitney Portal. Descending from Muir pass under headlight, I experienced a sudden sense of a penetrating peace. I was not alone. I was loved. Death was no longer an empty, dark abysmal morass.

Professionally, I am an ENT surgeon. Ironically, I was a physician who was so scared of death that I could not bring myself to consider my own mortality. With the infusion of the Holy Spirit, I was instantly cured of this hopelessness. It gave me a sudden realization that I could now face my fear of death and I understood the psychologic barriers that I had created to protect myself. My cure gave me insight about my own weakness. Although I was not worthy, God came under my roof and my soul was healed.

I have since come to the realization that the more dramatic the conversion story, the more embarrassing it becomes. I was so blind and oblivious that it took that much longer for me to hear and see. I now have great respect for those who grow in faith through a long slow, even, and persistent process. Three years later, during the Easter Vigil, I underwent the Catholic Rites of Initiation and entered communion with the Catholic Church.

My journey started with a personal experience. It took a lot of patience by my catechists to catch up what was then a fifty-two-year-old who was not only secular, but scientific! Before conversion, I was, in a profane sense, sin free. Now that I was awake, I was full of sin. Go figure—but I was learning the Truth. Now, things in the world that had been previously so confusing made perfect sense. Christianity was the cohesive and congruent framework that allowed me to understand the world.

I started teaching RCIA (Rites of Christian Initiation in Adults) when COVID hit, and, during a meeting outside in the park, Michael Eckstein showed for inquiry (a welcome distraction during the COVID pandemic). A Fundamentalist Baptist by upbringing, he was pursuing a Master of Arts degree in Christian Apologetics. Personally, I embrace the adage, "God does not call the qualified, He qualifies the called." I have enjoyed trying to keep up and ahead of you and your studies.

It was with great interest that I read the following manuscript. Michael's systematic approach to the topic of near-death experiences was reminiscent of how we med-students approached topics during medical school training. Intellectually, I never really gravitated to Apologetics as a vehicle for growing closer in Christ. I had started with a relationship with Christ and then, working backwards, learned about what that relationship meant.

In many ways, my experience tracks what near death experiences purvey—a deep penetrating permanent experience that can only be described using deeply religious language. Through Michael's work, I have gained an appreciation for the role of Apologetics in many Christians' lives. In truth, I wonder how long I get to discover new ways to demonstrate my naiveté. It is an open debate in my circles how long I can get by claiming to be a "new Catholic."

I especially enjoyed Michael's scholastic vigor and honest assessment of his subject matter. It appears he learned much along the way, following his lines of evidence to an unbiased conclusion. It is refreshing to encounter an honest approach during these highly subjective and agenda-oriented times. It also makes me curious about his treatment of eucharistic miracles, incorruptibility, and relics as an apologetic.

DR. PHIL WILEY, MD
DURANGO ENT

Preface

I HAVE ALWAYS LOVED the paranormal and the supernatural. As a child, my favorite holiday was Halloween, and I loved the feel of the cool evening air doing battle with the bonfire as I roasted marshmallows, the changing colors, and feeling that strange emptiness that settles across the world before the first snow. I especially loved the decorations, the costumes, and (especially) the books on the strange and mysterious that were everywhere that I turned.

As I grew up, that love never left me. Growing up mostly in Alaska, the stories of local haunts and of spirits that roamed the mountains (and the tundra) kept me fascinated. Spending summers in a small town in Germany that was located in a rather isolated part of a deep, dark wood, fairy tales seemed to come alive to me. Gathering with nearby friends and family, and trying to tell the scariest story, was always one of my favorite pastimes. Even today, living in the American southwest and doing ministry on a reservation, I encounter stories of Skinwalkers and vision quests.

I still love to watch videos of ghosts caught on tape. I want to visit houses where the dishes rattle at night and doors mysteriously open and close by themselves. When I hear the sound of a coyote outside at night, a part of me still thinks, "Chupacabra!"

Yet, I have always been quite a skeptic. I realize that seems to clash with what I have already said, but it is undeniably true. I knew inside that the voices of spirits were the wind and loneliness and isolation weighing heavily on those who ventured into the Alaskan wilderness. I could understand how the impenetrable darkness of the massive trees all around would lead people to get lost and even perish, and how the boars and wolves that made those German woods home would seem much bigger and greatly evil.

Typically, if you tell me you talked to Jesus in person last night, I most likely would ask if you had eaten something spicy for dinner. If you tell me your house is haunted, I most likely would ask if you have had someone come check for rodents. If you tell me that you died and had a deeply spiritual experience, I most likely would smile and nod, attributing the experience to a dying brain or an effect of medication. For me, near-death experiences were just another story of the paranormal: wonderful if true, but mostly likely just the creation of an active imagination.

It was a surprise to me when I came across near-death experiences in an academic setting. In the middle of a book about the case for the Resurrection of Jesus, there was an argument that near-death experiences could play an important role in making the larger case for the existence of God. The case was made by historian and New Testament theologian Gary Habermas, and he had decided to strip away all the elements of these experiences that could not be verified and focus on what doctors or family members corroborated. These accounts, Habermas believed, might be compelling to a naturalist.[1]

I, however, felt unsatisfied. I knew if anyone could make a compelling case for and from near-death experiences, it would be Habermas, but, at the end, I was simply not convinced of their authenticity. Still, I also realized the potential of near-death experiences in the argument for God's existence. Either they could bring people face-to-face with God's existence, or they would have to be tossed entirely. With that, I dove in. What follows is everything I found: the good and the bad regarding the intriguing tales and theories of near-death experiences.

---

1. Habermas, *The Risen Jesus*, 60–62.

Acknowledgments

FIRST, I WOULD LIKE to thank Dr. John S. Knox for his tireless efforts in making this work possible. Without his knowledge, insight, and experience, there is little doubt that these pages would be of far lesser quality. His boundless patience and eagerness to help certainly qualify him as a saint, even if only his students and God know it.

I also need to thank my brother, Mark, and sister, Michaela, who set aside time in their own studies to read and re-read this book. Their feedback helped keep things grounded rather than spiral into unhelpful academic minutiae. Their constant support, along with that of my parents, helped push me to the finish line.

Next, I must thank the spiritual leaders in my life: Dr. Phil Wiley, Fr. Cesar Arras, and Fr. Kevin Novack. As iron sharpens iron, these men have helped sharpen me in my spiritual life. Their faithful leadership helped me keep my focus on the One for whom we are working.

Finally, I want to thank my girls—Rowan and Piper. Their unwavering belief in their father was a constant reminder of what I can accomplish if I believed in myself just half as much as they believe in me.

1

Introduction

EVERY PERSON WILL EXPERIENCE the reality of death at some point in life. It is reasonable for anyone who faces the prospect of their own mortality to be uncomfortable or even afraid with its mystery. Still, many Christians have a hope of an afterlife in Heaven because of their belief that Jesus Christ died, rose from the grave, and ascended to Heaven. Naturalists, on the other hand, have no such hope for the future, for they believe that nothing beyond the natural realm exists and everything that exists must be able to be tested through the scientific method.[1]

In Western civilization, there exists a battle between these worldviews, and many naturalists feel that the burden of proof lies with the Christian in making this case against naturalism. As far as the naturalist can ascertain, there is only life and death, with death being the end of someone's existence. It would require positive proof that there is an afterlife in order for the naturalist to respond.

As Christians mount their case against naturalism, some people may ask themselves if death itself can be used as evidence. Can someone cross the barrier into death and come back to the living to describe an afterlife? Can accounts of this occurring, known as "near-death experiences," help tilt the scales in favor of Christianity? Because there is an apparent physical finality of death, it seems that the Christian apologist must turn to other arguments

---

1. Mortenson, "Religion of Naturalism," 206.

for Christianity and argue for the afterlife based on the truth of Christianity rather than rely on reports of near-death experiences to make his case.

American scholar and apologist Gary Habermas, however, believes that the Christian is not confined to taking this approach in believing in the afterlife. According to Habermas (who will have two entire chapters in this book dedicated to understanding and evaluating his apologetic of near-death experiences), near-death experiences pose such a challenge to the naturalist that he must abandon his basic worldview. Habermas says that naturalism itself then becomes an "illegitimate avenue" for rejecting the supernatural.[2] Habermas would acknowledge that this does not work as evidence towards the existence of God, but it opens up the possibility of an afterlife which the naturalist must grapple with.

This brings up many questions. Can Christians lean on near-death experiences as evidence for an afterlife? More importantly, should they? Douglas Groothuis writes, "Apologetics can be used to remove or diminish intellectual obstacles that hinder people from embracing Christ as Lord."[3] If this is the case, then the Christian's apologetic approach should remove that hindrance and not add to it. This standard is what will be used when examining the way Habermas uses near-death experiences in his apologetic works.

To show the influence near-death experiences can have on this debate, Habermas cites several atheist-philosophers who have acknowledged the challenges they pose. One such case is that of A. J. Ayer, who is unique among the philosophers discussed by Habermas because he had his own near-death experience, which Habermas suggested caused him to acknowledge the possibility of an afterlife.[4] Although one would be hard-pressed to make a case for an afterlife based on an individual's personal experience, a dramatic shift in someone's worldview can show the profundity of a near-death experience.

---

2. Habermas and Licona, *Case for Resurrection of Jesus*, 147.

3. Groothuis, *Christian Apologetics*, 28.

4. Habermas, *Risen Jesus and Future Hope*, 61.

According to Ayer, his experience with near-death involved seeing a bright light, angelic beings, and a distorted view of space and time. Although he stated that such near-death experiences could provide evidence that consciousness may exist after death, he denied that this would mean that there is a "future life," and he hypothesized that his brain continued to function even though he was dead.[5] Ayer wrote a follow-up article to re-emphasize his belief that his near-death experience was due to ongoing brain activity, despite the fact that he had been informed that brain activity had not been possible in his case.[6] In these articles, Ayer raised some important questions surrounding near-death experiences, particularly questions of what death is and how near-death experiences tie into it.

WHAT IS DEATH?

Death, being a guarantee for all living things, should be a fairly simple thing to define. After all, someone's death should be obvious. Potter Stewart famously wrote, "I know it when I see it."[7] However, though a precise definition will prove to be difficult, there are some standards used in the medical profession to confidently determine whether someone has died in cases where the certainty of death is more complicated.

Writing in the *British Journal of Nursing*, Bridgit Dimond described the issue with attempting to determine when someone is dead. The traditional way of determining death was simple enough: no breath and no pulse were all that was needed to declare someone dead. However, in a modern context in which machines can keep someone breathing and their heart beating artificially, a new definition has become necessary, which Dimond describes as coming in the form of assessing brain function.

A brain that is beyond functioning should be considered dead. In her use of using this definition for death, Dimond must include an important caveat. She wrote, "The possibility of brain death

5. Ayer, "What I Saw," 39.
6. Ayer, "Postscript to Postmortem."
7 Jacobellis v. Ohio, 378 U.S. 184 (1964).

should be used where the patient is deeply comatose (but where depressant drugs, primary hypothermia, and metabolic and endocrine disturbances can be excluded)."[8]

The problems with giving the term, "death," a specific definition should already be apparent. Death is the most obvious and inevitable aspect of life, but even a strict definition comes with exceptions to the rule. Dimond acknowledged some of the legal issues involved with using brain activity to determine death. Although written in the context of the British legal system, the implications seem to be valid, internationally. For families, seeing a loved one who is breathing and has a heartbeat removed from life support amounts to murder, even if the deceased brain has been "clinically dead" for some time. Even criminals have unsuccessfully attempted to evade murder charges by arguing that the actual death was caused by the doctors and not by the defendant.[9]

John Lizza represents a view on death that attempts to pull the definition away from being a strictly biological one. Lizza believes the issue is whether someone can regain consciousness. The permanent loss of consciousness marks the end of a human being, but not necessarily the end of an organism.[10] According to Lizza, because medical technology can allow an organism to continue to survive, the question of death must revolve around the personhood of the deceased.[11]

Steven Miles acknowledged the difficulties in the debate attempting to define death but believes this difficultly only needs to pertain to a few select cases of removing or retaining life support. Even in such cases, there should be no implication "that dying persons pass through an intermediate state between being alive and being dead."[12] For Miles, the debate should be centered on whether someone is dead or alive, and at what point death occurs—not whether there is something between life and death.

8. Dimond, "Clinical Definition," 391.
9. Dimond, "Clinical Definition," 392–93.
10. Lizza, "Defining Death," 9–10.
11. Lizza, "Defining Death," 10.
12. Miles, "Technological and Pluralistic Culture," 314.

The Christian view of death would generally agree with Miles on the lack of an intermediate state. There may be a variety of questions surrounding death that Christians across denominations may debate (such as the existence of Purgatory or if the soul is conscious after it leaves the body). There may also be a discussion of spiritual death and whether unrepentant souls are assigned eternal judgement, annihilation, or redemption. As confusing and hotly debated as these topics may be, physical death does not seem to be the root of controversy, and the question of whether someone is dead or alive remains the central issue. Most Christians are able to agree that death is to be "away from the body" (2 Corinthians 5:8).[13]

If what John Lizza described as "consciousness" can be attributed to the human soul as is the case in Christianity, there is no conflict with the idea of an organism remaining alive though the person has died. In using this language, there may be ethical concerns about when death occurs in regard to life support, but those concerns are beyond the scope of this book. However, as the debate over what death is continues to focus on the brain and consciousness, this has immediate implications for near-death experiences.

WHAT ARE NEAR-DEATH EXPERIENCES?

Figuring out how to accurately define near-death experiences can be a difficult endeavor. Much like finding a precise definition of what death is, near-death experiences can be subject to several definitions across a variety of experiences. According to Gary Habermas, evidential near-death experiences have "no measurable brainwaves or measurable heart-waves—they have that combination."[14] The fact that the standards for true death and near-death are so similar exposes the limitations in defining either, with the only apparent difference being whether or not the individual regains consciousness.

Near-death experiences are also surprisingly prevalent. According to Jeffrey Long, founder of the Near-Death Experience

---

13. Unless otherwise noted, all biblical passages referenced are in the *English Standard Version* (Wheaton: Crossway, 2008).

14. Cook et al., "What Happens," 05.

Foundation, there is no demographic that is more or less prone to having a near-death experience, and they are reported by 17% of those who "nearly die."[15] Age, gender, religious beliefs, and ethnicity do not seem to have any ramifications on whether an individual has this experience.[16] Raymond Moody reinforced the point on religious beliefs that "Many people with no prior interest or background in religion report powerful NDEs."[17] Furthermore, though each experience is unique, there are several characteristics of near-death experiences that are commonly reported.

Common Characteristics

According to Long, these experiences most commonly "include a perception of seeing and hearing apart from the physical body, passing into or through a tunnel, encountering a mystical light, intense and generally positive emotions, a review of part or all of their prior life experiences, encountering deceased loved ones, and a choice to return to their earthly life."[18] Moody affirmed these characteristics, clarifying that they almost always get reported in "the form of a travel narrative," suggesting that even if not each and every these common traits is experienced, there is still a common sequence to the event that can be expected and they are not randomly occurring events. An alternative to encountering a dark tunnel and a white light is an out-of-body experience in which the individual views themselves from outside their bodies, though it seems that both may occur.[19]

The frequency of each of these characteristics can vary. According to Charlotte Martial and others, by far the most common sequence of events includes the feeling of peace/bliss followed by encountering spirits or people. Most often, this feeling of peace will

15. Long, "Near-Death Experience," 372.
16. Long, "Near-Death Experience," 372.
17. Moody, "Getting Comfortable," 370.
18. Long, "Near-Death Experience," 372.
19. Moody, "Getting Comfortable," 369–70.

be preceded by an out-of-body experience.[20] Out-of-body experiences are reported by 45% of those who have been near-death. Research indicates that 92% of those who report out-of-body experiences were able to describe accurate events occurring in the same room or even at a great distance.[21]

The events surrounding near-death experiences are so integrated that it becomes difficult for the one with the experience to identify the order of the events. Martial suggests that these events may be "timeless," and the individuals' attempts to supply a sequence to the events may be a "temporal way of describing—or at least, time-distorted—experience."[22] This distortion of time is one of the hallmarks of a near-death when reflecting on the experience.[23]

As a way of explaining this distortion of time, John Fischer and Benjamin Mitchell-Yellin point to dreams and hallucinations. Just as dreams may feel like they take a long time to play out, the reality is that they most frequently occur in a few moments. Similarly, a LSD trip may "seem to last only a few minutes when in reality it lasted for hours."[24]

In this same way, a near-death experience can be completely distorted in time, creating the feeling of having the experience different from when the experience actually occurred.[25] However, people who have had near-death experiences typically deny that what they experienced has similarities to dreams, describing them as being "hyper-real"—more real than normal life.[26] According to Long, people describe seeing more colors, more details in what they see, and even a wider range of vision than in waking life. Even people blind from birth who have had a near-death experience describe sights and colors in vivid detail.[27]

20. Martial et al., "Temporality of Features," 7–8.

21. Long, "Near-Death Experience," 373–74.

22 Martial et al., "Temporality of Features," 7–8.

23. Cassol et al., "Qualitative Thematic Analysis," 9.

24. Fischer and Mitchell-Yellin, *Near-Death Experiences*, 17–18.

25 Fischer and Mitchell-Yellin, *Near-Death Experiences*, 17–18.

26. Moody, "Getting Comfortable," 370.

27. Long, "Near-Death Experience," 373–75.

Yet, Fischer and Mitchell-Yellin remain skeptical. Turning again to dreams, drugs, and hallucinations, they point out that what someone experiences in any of these situations may certainly feel real, and they are indeed real experiences. This does not mean that they are "accurate experiences."[28] When it comes to the visual experiences of the blind, they do not put much stock in these claims either. Describing the two types of blindness that occur they claim that both have reasonable natural explanations.

In the first type, "no-input blindness," the eyes do not function properly, and therefore cannot see. In such cases, the eyes can still have "visual impressions" and can even have accurate visual experiences that show up in near-death experiences. The second type, "processing blindness," would provide a much more compelling case for supernaturalism in near-death experiences, though it is far less common. In this case, the brain cannot process any visual impressions, and therefore is a deeper level of blindness.[29] They feel that this too will have a physical explanation, but the fact that most accounts of the blind seeing during near-death experiences do not signify which type of blindness the individual has, and the fact that "no-input blindness" is far more common, this overall does not help the case for supernaturalism in near-death experiences.[30]

According to Moody, upon waking, people find that they have an entirely new outlook on life. Past goals and priorities change. Thereafter, they find "that the most important goal in life is to learn to love." Their new focus is on an afterlife they are now convinced exists.[31] According to Gary Habermas, many people do not want to go back to their lives, sometimes even fighting off the doctor who is resuscitating them.[32] Many report being given a choice by an entity as to whether they will go back, and in nearly all cases, they would prefer to stay but go back for the sake of others.[33]

28. Fischer and Mitchell-Yellin, *Near-Death Experiences*, 35.

29. Fischer and Mitchell-Yellin, *Near-Death Experiences*, 50–52.

30. Fischer and Mitchell-Yellin, *Near-Death Experiences*, 58–60.

31. Moody, "Getting Comfortable," 370.

32. Cook et al., "What Happens," 28:24.

33 Moody, "Getting Comfortable," 370.

Although feelings of peace and a desire to stay away from the physical body are commonly reported, that is not to say that these experiences are universal or that there are no negative near-death experiences. Feelings of peace may be the most often reported, but each experience is unique, and a variety of emotions have been described, such as "astonishment, amazement, surprise, and fear."[34] Habermas describes some of these experiences as being "distressing," and they account for 21% of all near-death experiences.[35]

Distressing Near-Death Experiences

Nancy Bush and Bruce Greyson observed three types of distressing near-death experiences. The first, called "inverse" experiences, report most of the same events that are reported in a typical near-death experience, but they are perceived by the individual as being distinctly negative. The same events which others described as being wonderful are then described by these individuals as being terrifying and depressing, such as finding themselves helpless to do anything about what appears to be happening to them.[36]

The second type, "void" experiences, also share some of the characteristics of typical near-death experiences, though the similarities are less of a focus than with inverse experiences. They are typically accompanied by a sense of emptiness and hopelessness. There is darkness without a tunnel of light or a great sense of emptiness and hopelessness. There may also be interactions with spiritual beings, but they are cruel rather than loving.[37]

Bush and Greyson describe a third type of near-death experience that they believe to be the least common, although it is certainly the most interesting. This experience is called a "hellish" near-death experience, and the name is certainly apt. These experiences often involve visits to what the individual believes is Hell, seeing and hearing spirits in torment, and even the sensation of being

34. Cassol et al., "Qualitative Thematic Analysis," 10–11.
35. Cook et al., "What Happens," 27:05.
36. Bush and Greyson, "Distressing Near-Death Experiences," 486.
37. Bush and Greyson, "Distressing Near-Death Experiences," 487.

attacked by demonic creatures.[38] It is this category of distressing near-death experiences that seems to provide fodder for television, movies, and books.

Helena Cassol and others did follow-up research into distressing near-death experiences based on work done by Bush and Greyson. Using a sample size of 506 participants, they estimated that approximately 14% of near-death experiences were distressing, as opposed to Habermas's estimate of 21%.[39] They also had different numbers from Greyson and Bush when it came to the frequency of the types of distressing experiences. Greyson and Bush suggested that inverse experiences are the most common, followed by void experiences, and lastly, hellish experiences were a rarity.[40] The follow-up research indicated that inverse and hellish experiences occurred with similar frequency and void experiences occurred far less frequently than either of the others.[41] Although there were some discrepancies in the numbers from what other researchers have shown, most of what Bush and Greyson described was confirmed by this research, and it points to the need for more research to be done in the area of distressing near-death research beyond what is described as "classical" near-death experiences.[42]

Just as there are three types of distressing near-death experiences, Bush and Greyson describe three different reactions people tend to have after their near-death experiences. A common response is a change in outlook. People begin to pick up positive behaviors and leave negative ones behind. Many become religious or dive deeper into their religions. Although it seems to be similar to a typical positive near-death experience in which people seek to live better and more loving lives, these turnarounds after having a negative experience tend to have a lingering feeling of fear afterward.[43]

---

38. Bush and Greyson, "Distressing Near-Death Experiences," 487.

39. Cassol et al., "Systematic Analysis of Distressing," 3–4.

40. Bush and Greyson, "Distressing Near-Death Experiences," 486–87.

41 Cassol et al., "Systematic Analysis of Distressing," 4.

42. Cassol et al., 7.

43. Bush and Greyson, "Distressing Near-Death Experiences," 487.

The second response is to attempt to brush off the event. The event will be ignored, or the individual will rationalize what they experienced. Some will turn to biological explanations or blame it on the hospital medications in order to avoid allowing any "ontological meaning" to the event and "any lingering anxieties will go unaddressed."[44] Bush and Greyson believe that even if these explanations are correct, the mental effects the near-death experience had on someone need to be addressed and should not merely be dismissed.

The third response is labeled by Bush and Greyson as "the long haul" response. Unlike those who change their outlooks on life, those who have this response seem to have difficulty knowing how to process their distressing near-death experience. Unlike those who attempt to simply brush off their experience, these individuals are not satisfied with a mere biological explanation for how their experience occurred. Instead, they are haunted by what they saw and felt, looking for psychological relief through therapy.

While those who have a change in outlook will often turn to religion, "long haul" individuals will often distance themselves from religion, feeling that God would not or could not help, or he simply was not there. While the typical positive near-death experience can reduce the individual's fear of death and may even cause him to look forward to it, the distressing experience can have a lingering fear of death that may never go away.[45]

Bush and Greyson believe that distressing near-death experiences are widely underreported due to the intense negative emotions and sometimes trauma associated with them; however, there are still things that can be learned from these experiences. Much like a typical near-death experience, a distressing experience seems to be unrelated to someone's gender, age, or religious beliefs. Lifestyle does not seem to have any effect on whether the experience is a positive or negative one. Regardless of how someone responds (or attempts to respond) to a distressing experience, the experience

---

44 Bush and Greyson, "Distressing Near-Death Experiences," 488.

45. Bush and Greyson, "Distressing Near-Death Experiences," 488–89.

typically "overturns experiencers' personal life and social relationships abruptly and permanently."[46]

For the medical community, dealing with the experiences of these patients and their families poses another problem. Ideally, medical professionals can deal with their patients in a clinical way, and near-death experiences remove the inherently more naturalistic nature of medicine. Ultimately, it may be best for the doctor to step away from the clinical and material mindset. According to Bush and Evans, "Non-judgmental listening may be the most workable alternative."[47]

HISTORICAL NEAR-DEATH EXPERIENCES

It would be difficult to argue that using near-death experiences as evidence for an afterlife would not work because of lack of interest. Near-death experiences and the stereotypical characteristics of them are all over popular media, and near-death experiences make for a lucrative story for which the public eagerly pays, arguably peaking with the film, *Heaven Is for Real*, based on the book by the same name, which made over $101 million,[48] while the book itself sold over ten million copies.[49] Contemporary fiction and nonfiction alike are replete with examples of near-death experiences, and the financial payoffs of them.

Contemporary Interest

For Christians, much of the interest in near-death experiences comes in the form of "Heaven tourism" books, a term made popular by Tim Challies in his discussion of whether people have actually seen Heaven while having a near-death experience.[50] Challies rejected all such claims outright, citing the great financial incentive

46. Bush and Greyson, "Distressing Near-Death Experiences," 490.
47. Bush and Greyson, "Distressing Near-Death Experiences," 490.
48. Dedrick, "Why are Christians Fascinated?"
49. Johnson, "Heaven Is for Real"
50. Dedrick, "Why are Christians Fascinated?"

that can come with these books as being the reason for the existence of any such books being sold at all. It should be noted, however, that Challies does not believe in the authenticity of accounts regarding near-death experiences outside of being a psychological event. He seems to reference Hebrews 9:27 in his rejection of near-death experiences when he wrote, "The Bible says that it is for man to die once and then to experience the resurrection."[51] Although not an authority on the subject, Challies' opinion on the matter seems to reflect common popular criticism of Heavenly and near-death experiences, and he has had an influence in the dialogue about them.

Challies' concerns about these "Heaven tourism" books are certainly not without merit. Although not reaching the incredible heights of *Heaven Is for Real*, the book, *The Boy Who Came Back From Heaven*, managed to sell over a million copies, and the initial success of the book opened the door for many of the other "Heaven tourism" books that followed.[52]

Five years later, Alex Malarkey, who co-authored the book with his father, wrote an open letter to Lifeway through the online blog *Pulpit and Pen*, admitting that the entire story was fabricated and being used to make money, and he called on the publisher to remove the book from print. Although he was indeed near-death due to a car accident, he did not see Heaven, nor did he have a sensory near-death experience.[53]

Although it appears that the unfortunate case of Malarkey may have caused a slump in the "Heaven tourism" fad, a completely cynical view of near-death would be unfair. Christian audiences also showed a continued interest in near-death Heaven experiences as only a year after Malarkey's open letter (which had become widely publicized) *Miracles from Heaven*, another "Heaven tourism" film made nearly seventy-four million dollars against a budget of approximately thirteen million.[54]

---

51. Challies, "Heaven Tourism."
52. Graham, "I Did Not Die."
53 Malarkey and The News Division, "Boy Who Came Back."
54. "Miracles from Heaven (2016)."

Interest in near-death experiences amongst the general population is quite high as well. It is frequently a topic of news stories, as, for example, on August 25, 2020, a woman detailed her own personal near-death experience in an online newspaper, which the reporter followed up with an opinion from a medical doctor who specialized in resuscitation research.[55] Examples in the same vein abound. It is also a frequent focus of "pop culture" magazines and at the summer blockbuster.

One Irish biochemist wrote a popular article describing near-death experiences and indicating that both popular and scientific interest in the subject may be reaching an all-time high as "research on NDEs is very active."[56] Although the number of people not identifying with any religious denomination has increased dramatically over the past decade, those who still identify as "spiritual" makes up a large part of that demographic,[57] further emphasizing the relevance of seemingly spiritual experiences in apologetics.

Near-Death Experiences in History

Although public interest in near-death experiences seems to be a uniquely modern phenomenon, descriptions of these experiences have been reported throughout history. As discussed above, knowing precisely when someone is dead is notoriously difficult, and in a world where brain activity was impossible to monitor, defining death would seem to be much simpler yet would inherently be far less accurate. The changes in the body after death that were not recognized as decomposition were believed to be signs of life (and the bodies were quickly desecrated in order to avoid potential plagues, particularly of the undead variety).[58]

As previously discussed, death is not always a clear thing, and mistakes happen even today. On March 3, 2021, a man in India was declared dead and removed from life support. It was not until

55. Martin, "Near Death Experience."
56. Reville, "Near Death Experience."
57. Saunders et al., "Religious (Non)Affiliation," 424–30.
58 Barber, "The Real Vampire," 55.

the mortician was about to start an autopsy that the man moved his body, and it became clear that he was still alive.[59] First world countries are not immune either. On March 13, 2021, a man in England was declared brain dead and was scheduled to have his organs harvested. With his sister's encouragement, he was able to twitch his body. Less than two weeks later, he was breathing on his own.[60]

If such mistakes can happen today, then before the age of modern medicine the possibility of reviving from a death-like state was far more likely, and it was a reality that people went through great lengths to avoid. Larry Dossey, writing on fears of being buried alive, describes a variety of accounts in which people had appeared to be dead, were buried, and later discovered to have revived in their coffins only to suffocate or starve. Most of these stories are simply horrifying, almost always ending with a true death for the individual while those who were able to avoid that fate were generally unaware of what was happening. Such accounts were so prevalent that those who could afford to do so took precautions to avoid this fate, including providing ways to end their own lives in case of being buried alive.

In a memorable story, a young woman was accused of murder and hung for thirty minutes, then buried. A doctor in need of a cadaver dug her up and was observant enough to notice that she inhaled. After a few days of intensive care, she recovered, with no memory of any of the events.[61]

In these scenarios, both contemporary and historical, there is no mention of a near-death experience even as they all seem to fit into the wider debate over what death is, as discussed above. Although the reasons why could be speculated upon, the fact that only 17% of people who nearly die report having a near-death experience[62] should create the expectation that most people who resuscitate will not have an experience to discuss, at least none they will remember. History will, however, provide stories that include

59. French-Presse, "'Dead' Man Comes Alive."
60. Vincent, "Incredible Moment Teenager."
61. Dossey, "The Undead," 347–48.
62. Long, "Near-Death Experience," 372.

near-death experiences which match the common traits that have been discussed.

One very early, and arguably the most famous, account of a near-death experience comes from Plato's *The Republic*. Plato describes a young man, Er, who was killed in battle and prepared on a pyre to be burned. Er had an out-of-body experience, encountered various spiritual beings, saw a divine judgement with visions of torture and blessings, felt deeply peaceful, and went down a tunnel of light. Er appears to hit the most common major elements of a near-death experience, with the exception of knowing how he returned to his body.[63]

In the ancient east and near-east, near-death experiences are more frequently reported, although usually in a religious context. Possibly the earliest account of a near-death experience comes from ancient Mesopotamia. It included an out-of-body experience, interactions with angelic beings, reuniting with deceased relatives, and a return to the living.[64]

Ancient China has several similar accounts (with one source claiming as many as 127), although there are often mythological elements mixed in with what is typically reported of near-death experiences. There are, however, several reports that are more straightforward. One such example reports an individual who was sick, had a vision of Heaven, and returned with supposedly verified information about future events. Another account is of a woman who was thought to be dead for six days, during which she interacted with her deceased father who then sent her back to her body.[65]

Crossing the ocean to ancient Mesoamerica, one finds more reports of near-death experiences. One report hits almost every characteristic of a typical near-death experience, including "elements of out-of-body journeys to other realms, a guide, a sense of joy (singing; presents brought by the guide), other spirits and deceased relatives, idealized mirror-image of earth, encountering a divine/supernatural presence (Tlaloc), and a return characterized

---

63. Plato, *The Republic*, bk. 10.

64. Shushan, *Conceptions of Afterlife*, 167–68.

65. Shushan, *Conceptions of Afterlife*, 168.

by a positive transformation." Other reports include a woman who was revived and made prophecies based on what she experienced.[66]

The earliest known medical report of a near-death experience comes from the early eighteenth century. Though reports of near-death experiences are much older, as demonstrated above, this report would be the first to be considered a "medical" report in the modern sense. The description from the physician included a loss of physical senses, seeing a white light which the individual felt was the entrance to Heaven, a feeling of peace, and an encounter with an angelic being.[67]

Moving to the Industrial Era (around 1791), British naval officer Sir Francis Beaufort describes a drowning near-death experience in a written account. He details an overwhelming feeling of bliss and then seeing his life play out in reverse, as it "seemed to be placed before me in a kind of panoramic view."[68] In 1900, a doctor suffering from fever described leaving his body and having feelings of peace, not wanting to return to his body. He had this experience several times throughout the duration of his fever.[69]

In 1918, one of the quintessential authors of American literature, Ernest Hemingway, had his own near-death experience when he was nineteen years old. After being seriously wounded on his head by shrapnel, Hemingway had the experience of leaving his body but quickly returned. Rather than feeling peaceful about death after this experience, he spent the rest of his life worried that he would die again, especially when he slept. He would repeatedly play out this experience in his fiction, describing near-death experiences in much the same way as contemporary sources.[70]

66. Shushan, *Conceptions of Afterlife*, 168.

67. Charlier, "Oldest Medical Description," e155.

68. Koch, "Tales of Dying Brain," 35–36.

69. Koch, "Tales of Dying Brain."

70. Vardamis and Owens, "Ernest Hemingway," 203–4.

SUMMARY

The apparent interest in near-death experiences spans across human history, and today's technology, where information can be sent across the world in the blink of an eye, has only increased that interest. Whether they are aimed at giving hope to the religious for a future in Heaven or to titillate people's fascination with the supernatural, books, magazines, and films are quick to leave the shelves. Although it can seem to some that (despite their universal characteristics across time and geography) studying near-death experiences may be a shallow pursuit. However, it is important to remember from where that fascination comes.

Everyone has to face the reality of their own death. Gary Habermas pointed to atheists like Anthony Flew and A. J. Ayers and the impact near-death experiences (whether reported or personal) had on them and their beliefs.[71] Habermas is certainly correct in this, as the reality is when it comes to facing death, the typical atheist is more receptive of ideas about the supernatural than he would be otherwise.

In a series of studies published in the *Journal of Experimental Social Psychology*, researchers found that when confronted with their own mortality, theists and atheists alike would double down on their explicitly stated beliefs. However, when measured implicitly, belief in the supernatural increased—regardless of what the stated explicit belief was. For atheists and skeptics, the difference between the participants and the control group was large enough to be significant.[72] This demonstrates that even a verbally strident naturalist will be concerned with his or her own impending death. Nonaggressive apologetics in this area can have the effect of at least making the naturalist consider the importance of what may lie behind death, and near-death experiences can certainly provide a line of reasoning to point in that direction.

---

71. Habermas, *Risen Jesus and Future Hope*, 61.
72. Jong, Halberstadt, and Bluemke, "Foxhole Atheism," 986–87.

2

Research

AS PREVIOUSLY DISCUSSED, THOSE who endure a near-death experience tend to have many commonalities in what they see, hear, and feel. Whether the experience is positive or negative (or Hellish), many of the elements remain the same: spiritual visions, spiritual beings, intense emotions, and so on. The aftermath of these events often involves common personal changes in the lives of individuals. Although reports tend to be scant, there have been reports of near-death experiences throughout history, the details of which line up with what is reported in modern accounts.

These experiences certainly appear to have a spiritual dimension and Gary Habermas's example of A. J. Ayer shows that even an atheist can have the impression of having had a spiritual experience. Habermas even pointed to atheist Anthony Flew conceding that near-death experiences seem to indicate a separation from the conscious mind and the physical body.[1] What then needs to be asked is what sort of research exists on what occurs biologically during a near-death experience and how those effects manifest themselves, psychologically. If such things are entirely explained by biology or human psychology, then there is little meaning behind what the individual may feel that he has experienced or the life changes that he has made other than the positive experience in the individual's own life.

1. Habermas and Licona, *Case for Resurrection of Jesus*, 147.

SEEING THE LIGHT

BIOLOGICAL

One study from the early 2000s chose to look exclusively at occurrences of near-death experiences in those who have had cardiac
arrest. Cardiac arrest was chosen as the medical criteria because it
can be an objectively defined medical situation. The research was
limited to Dutch hospitals and to patients who suffered cardiac
arrest, were clinically dead, and had undergone cardiopulmonary
resuscitation.[2]

Everyone who was surveyed was interviewed within a few
days of their medical experience. Along with being asked about
the specifics of their medical experiences (such as where CPR was
performed and how often they were resuscitated), the participants
were also asked about whether they had a previous near-death experience or had even heard of near-death experiences. With whom-
ever possible, there was a follow-up interview with participants two
years after their initial experience and a second follow-up eight
years afterward. There was also a control group that matched the
demographics of those interviewed but did not report any sort of
near-death experience.[3]

As was expected by the researchers, most of these patients
did not report any sort of near-death experience. The researchers
believed that this helped to limit several common explanations for
these experiences. If they could be accounted for by hallucinations
due to lack of oxygen to the brain as the body is clinically dead, then
the number of people with these experiences should be much higher.
Medications in the treatment also did not seem to have any correlation to whether the individual had a near-death experience. The
brain reacting out of fear was also ruled out as it seemed not to be
associated with whether someone has had a near-death experience.

Age did seem to be significant in whether someone reported
a near-death experience. Younger people tended to report the experience with more frequency than those who were older. This also
seems to line up with the fact that younger people (particularly
those under sixty) were more likely to survive having a heart attack

2. Lommel et al., "Near-Death Experience in Survivors," 2039–40.
3. Lommel et al., "Near-Death Experience in Survivors," 2040.

than those who were older. Short-term memory also played a role in whether someone reported a near-death experience, with people who have memory defects being less likely to report an experience.

Although the researchers believed that their study helped rule out a lot of explanations for near-death experiences, they held to the idea that there is a scientific explanation for what occurs and is experienced. While they did not believe that the brain itself can cause them (since in most reported cases there is no brain activity), they believed that consciousness could function apart from the functions of the human body, and research should focus on these areas.[4]

In keeping with cardiac arrest, another study attempted to expand on the above research and explored the effect of carbon dioxide on near-death experiences for those who survived cardiac arrest. In addition, it looked at the possible effects of potassium and sodium in the blood. Although it also looked at cardiac arrest survivors, there were areas of research that had so far been unexplored and some where the researchers appear to have tried to explore these areas.

The researchers focused on cardiac arrest survivors who were resuscitated outside of the hospital and then taken to intensive care. Each patient had to be over the age of eighteen and had to be clinically dead (as defined by heart rather than brain activity) at the time of their near-death experience. The research was done in primarily three hospitals in Slovenia, limiting the scope of the research.[5]

The research indicated a strong correlation between the level of carbon dioxide measured and whether a near-death experience occurs. Although there is some question as to when the experience occurs, the researchers believed that these experiences occurred during the cardiac arrest itself. Because high levels of carbon dioxide can have strong hallucinogenic effects, the researchers believed that it may play an important role in whether someone has a near-death experience. Lower levels of potassium were found in those who had intense near-death experiences, but the information was not statistically significant enough to suggest a correlation.[6]

---

4. Lommel et al., "Near-Death Experience," 2043–44.
5. Klemenc-Ketis, Kersnik, and Grmec, "Effect of Carbon Dioxide," 1–2.
6. Klemenc-Ketis, Kersnik, and Grmec, "Effect of Carbon Dioxide," 4–5.

Although most attributes of a typical near-death experience were confirmed by the study, others were not. This apparent discrepancy, however, was attributed to the smaller and limited sample size of the study. From the study, the researchers concluded that the two most important factors in determining whether someone would have a near-death experience were the level of carbon dioxide in their blood and whether the individual had a previous near-death experience.[7]

Researchers Willoughby B. Britton and Richard R. Bootzin studied the brain activity in the temporal lobe of those who have reported a near-death experience and compared it to those who suffer from PTSD after experiencing "life-threatening trauma" as well as temporal-lobe epileptics. Their expectations were that those with near-death experiences would have positive post-experience reactions dissimilar from those with PTSD but similar to those with epilepsy due to altered central lobe function.[8] Just as those who have had near-death experiences tend to develop positive outlooks and become more religious,[9] those who had epileptic seizures go through a similar adjustment of changing emotions, outlook, and religion as epileptic seizures can create what appear to be deeply religious experiences.[10]

Britton and Bootzin's research included forty-three participants across a variety of forms of trauma: "Life-threatening events included accidents (43.5%), medical complications (17.4%), heart attacks (17.5%), allergic reactions (8.7%), and suicide attempts (8.7%). Head trauma was sustained in 21.7% of the accidents."[11] The control group was matched demographically to the participants in the trauma group, but without a history of life-threatening experiences, seizures, a family history of epilepsy, or sleep problems (as verified by a sleep study of the participants). Essentially, Britton

---

7. Klemenc-Ketis, Kersnik, and Grmec, "Effect of Carbon Dioxide," 5–6.

8. Britton, and Bootzin, "Near-Death Experiences," 254.

9 Bush and Greyson, "Distressing Near-Death Experiences," 487.

10. Presinger, "Religious and Mystical Experiences," 1257–58.

11 Britton and Bootzin, "Near-Death Experiences," 254–55.

and Bootzin screened for anything in the medical history of the participants that could cause abnormal temporal lobe functioning.

Britton and Bootzin, having expected the abnormalities to be found on the right side of the temporal lobe, were surprised when this turned out not to be the case. With a single exception, all abnormal activity of the study group occurred on the left side. Along with having this higher abnormal brain activity, the study group and control group showed significant differences during their sleep studies. The study group tended to sleep an hour less than the control group, reached REM sleep later in the night, and had fewer periods of REM sleep. Despite these differences, both groups averaged the same percentage (in minutes) of REM sleep through the night.[12]

The study group was found to be significantly better at using positive coping mechanisms and experiencing personal growth than the control group. There was not a significant difference in negative coping mechanisms. Such differences between the study and control groups, however, "May represent a neurophysiological difference between traumatized and nontraumatized [sic] individuals rather than something unique to those who have had near-death experiences."

Despite acknowledging this difference, Britton and Bootzin indicate that there is good reason to believe that their findings may be unique to near-death experience survivors rather than trauma survivors in general. When comparing the results of the sleep study to the research of other survivors of traumatic experiences, the results seemed unique to those who had a near-death experience. Unlike those with PTSD or dissociative disorders, who tend to have "negative stress reactions," those with near-death experiences tended to have positive coping mechanisms. What is not clear to the researchers is whether there is a pre-existing condition that causes a near-death experience that is absent from others.[13]

The connection between near-death experiences and REM sleep would be further explored by Daniel Kondziella, Jens P. Dreier, and Markus Harboe Olsen. They created a study to see if there

12. Britton and Bootzin, "Near-Death Experiences," 254–55.

13 Britton and Bootzin, "Near-Death Experiences," 256–58.

was a connection between REM sleep intrusion (meaning the experience of rapid eye movement and having dreams while in a state of wakefulness) and having a near-death experience. They based their research on a previous study that seemed to suggest REM intrusion was an underlying cause to many of the characteristics of a near-death experience.[14]

The researchers of this previous study seemed to believe that because REM intrusion is both relatively common (and underlies various other conditions such as narcolepsy), it may be an underlying prerequisite to having a near-death experience. They also believed that this may be more prevalent in those with cardiorespiratory conditions and that they tied in with human flight-or-fight responses.[15]

Unfortunately, this research was met with criticism. Researchers Jeffrey Long and Janice Minor Holden seem to believe that almost all the claims made by the researchers in the study were overstated and not supported well enough to merit them. The biggest problems that they had with the survey had to do with the questions the survey asked and the participants themselves. Regarding the questions, first, the question on sleep intrusion may have been too broad, overstating the number of people who reported having sleep intrusion. Then, the question did not distinguish whether these experiences occurred before or after their near-death experience, but rather they assumed the former. Lastly, the questions on REM intrusion may not reveal a greater predisposition to near-death experiences for those that have REM intrusion but perhaps a greater awareness of them after having a near-death experience.[16]

When it came to issues with participant selection, Long and Holden first found that the questions allowed for anyone who had experienced a life-threatening situation to have unusual sleep patterns—not merely those who had an accompanying near-death experience. Second, the control group was made up of medical personnel and may, therefore, have been more cautious in answering

14. Kondziella, Dreier, and Olsen, "Prevalence of Near-Death," e7585.

15. Nelson et al., "Does the Arousal System Contribute?" 1005–1006.

16. Long and Holden, "Does the Arousal System Contribute," 143–44.

the survey questions. Third, the participants may have represented a subset of those with near-death experiences who would have been more likely to be aware of REM intrusion in their lives. Lastly, they feared the researchers may have eliminated some of those participants who could have affected the outcomes.[17]

Kondziella, Dreier, and Olsen wanted to avoid the mistakes made by the previous study, and so they took the words of the response paper to heart. They made the only requirements of participants to be that they spoke English and were over the age of eighteen. To ensure honesty from participants, the researchers assured them that their monetary compensation was fixed regardless of whether they reported having a near-death experience or not. For anyone who reported not having a near-death experience, their participation in the study ended. If the participant responded that they had such an experience, they were asked in-depth questions to measure the viability of their experience. Participants were then asked about associated negative feelings (which is not typically covered in near-death experience surveys), and then were able to describe their experiences in their own words.[18]

They found that there is a significant correlation between REM sleep intrusion and near-death experiences. They found that "Sleep-related visual and auditory hallucinations and/or sleep paralysis. . . were substantially more common in cases with near-death experiences."[19] They believed that this REM sleep intrusion could explain why some people have actual auditory and visual hallucinations when near death. Even when adjusting for things such as age, gender, etc., this correlation remained significant.[20]

As discussed above, it must be pointed out that those who have a near-death experience can readily point to features that are quite unlike dreams. Instead, they suggest that their experiences feel real, even "hyper-real" compared to even waking life.[21] Colors

17. Long and Holden, "Does the Arousal System Contribute," 148.

18. Kondziella, Dreier, and Olsen, "Prevalence of Near-Death," 1–3.

19. Kondziella, Dreier, and Olsen, "Prevalence of Near-Death," 9–10.

20. Kondziella, Dreier, and Olsen, "Prevalence of Near-Death," 12.

21 Moody, "Getting Comfortable with Death," 370.

are brighter, details more vivid, and even blind people report visual experiences.[22] If near-death experiences are significantly different from dreaming, then even the prevalence of REM sleep and sleep intrusion during wakefulness do not suggest that they are the same or even similar.

Following up on their work done with REM sleep studies, the members of the previous research team composed a follow-up study that investigated migraines with auras to determine whether they may be indicators of a future near-death experience. Pointing to previous studies, the researchers believed that the connections between REM sleep and migraines are numerous, as people who experience migraines tend to have vivid dreams, migraine attacks often happen during REM sleep, and they have more REM sleep and have REM latency. They also believed that another possible connection is between migraines and REM intrusion. This led the researchers to ask whether migraine auras were indicative of people having near-death experiences.[23]

One previous study used was by Harold Levitan, who found that migraines often occurred during REM sleep, particularly during nightmares. While waking migraines are common, they are usually set off by feelings of frustration, whereas those that occur from dreams usually involve a sense of terror.[24] Another showed that hallucinations are often associated with migraines, both visual (usually with migraine aura) and even olfactory.[25]

The researchers used an online survey platform to reach an international audience, with the only requirements to participate being that the participant could read English and was not involved in their previous study. They offered twenty cents as payment for participation. General questions on the survey included age, gender, employment, etc., while more specific questions were whether the participants experienced long headaches that were accompanied by "visual or non-visual aura," as well as questions regarding

22. Long, "Near-Death Experience," 373–75.

23. Kondziella et al., "Migraine Aura," 2–3.

24 Levitan, "Dreams Which Culminate," 165–66.

25 Daniel and Donnet, "Migrainous Complex Hallucinations," 999–1001.

any previous near-death experiences while there were no questions regarding REM sleep. The researchers evaluated all reported near-death experiences—regardless of whether they were reported as being in a truly life-threatening situation or not.

Out of the 1,037 participants that were recruited, some 286 reported having a near-death experience. Most of those who reported a near-death experience reported having many of their common attributes, such as an altered sense of time and "vivid sensations," and just less than half reported an out-of-body experience. However, only eighty-one of the participants ultimately met the criteria of having had such an experience.[26]

Traditional surveys regarding migraines were lacking in several areas. Usually, they had to be done by a neurologist, which made the process difficult and costly. Alternatives that had been developed for researchers did not consider migraines with auras or headache-free participants. Therefore, a branching logic questionnaire was developed to easily distinguish among those with various levels of severity of their headaches as well as their history of headaches and family history of headaches. The survey even asked if the participants took the questions seriously or if their answers should be discarded.[27]

The researchers followed this more precise test to see who met these criteria when surveying participants. Although 720 people reported headaches not attributed to illness nor injury, there were only 254 people having experienced migraine aura, though these were across various types of auras. Of these, thirty-three percent were women and fifteen percent were men, a difference that the researchers called "statistically significant."[28] Those with migraine auras also tended to skew older than those who did not. Meanwhile, there was no significant difference between genders or age groups when it came to having a near-death experience.

The percentage of participants (8%) that had a near-death experience fell within the expected range of the general population.

26. Kondziella et al., "Migraine Aura," 5–7.
27. Kaiser et al., "Branching Logic Questionnaire," 1257–58.
28. Kondziella et al., "Migraine Aura," 8.

Unlike the common theme across near-death experience research that they are almost always pleasant or even euphoric experiences, this study found higher levels of negative experiences. Those who had a more negative near-death experience usually scored lower on the researchers' test on whether a near-death experience occurred.[29]

It was clear in their findings that there was a correlation between migraines with auras and near-death experiences. This remained true whether there were adjustments for variables such as sex or age. The researchers acknowledge that because they put the fact that they were researching near-death experiences and headaches into the internet announcement, they may have inadvertently selected a higher population of people who have had near-death experiences and headaches, including those with migraines with auras.

Although these numbers were higher than was expected based on other migraine studies, the ratio of those who experienced migraines with auras, which is approximately twice as likely in females, was within expectations. They believed that "future non-internet-based studies will therefore be necessary to verify that NDE and migraine aura are indeed associated," even as they believed their online survey helped prevent bias and was able to reach a more diverse sample of participants.[30]

Once again, the difficulty in truly defining "death" becomes apparent in the discussion of the survey, as the researchers briefly describe the neurobiology of death for them to make their connections between migraines and near-death experiences, which are typically characterized by four things. Describing these, they wrote, "The transition from life to death is thus characterized by four major events: loss of circulation, loss of respiration, loss of spontaneous electrocorticography (ECoG) activity, and a terminal SD [spreading depolarization] without repolarization."[31]

Death then occurs in four phases, but it is in the second phase in which electrocorticography activity is no longer detectable. According to the researchers, this is not because of the lack of brain

29. Kondziella et al., "Migraine Aura," 8–9.

30 Kondziella et al., "Migraine Aura," 11–12.

31. Kondziella et al., "Migraine Aura," 13.

activity but rather an overload of synaptic activity. They point to other areas of sleep study that show similar events occur during REM sleep, and this may be a key point in future research for the cause of near-death experiences.

The researchers speculated that it is during the spreading depolarization of the brain that the bright light or "tunnel vision" may occur because the way it occurs is similar to what people experience when they have a migraine with an aura. While all people will experience spreading depolarization when they die, "People with a propensity for migraine aura may be more likely to experience terminal SD while the brain is still electrically active."[32] Therefore, it appears the terminal spreading depolarization can be remembered, as in the cases of near-death experiences.

The researchers drew a dark conclusion from their survey regarding organ donation. Because many medical facilities will immediately begin organ harvesting after death, the organ harvesting may be premature as the terminal spreading depolarization may be reversible, which the researchers suggest is the case with near-death experiences. Further research in this area has the potential to save lives from dramatic medical errors as the medical community expands its understanding of death. Because abnormal REM sleep is associated with migraines, and both narcolepsy and hallucinations are associated with migraines with aura, it seems that these then are indicators of whether someone will have a near-death experience and may give a broader understanding of death.[33]

PSYCHOLOGICAL

Some of the previously examined research studied the connection between REM sleep and near-death experiences. Although an area such as dreaming can skirt the border of biological and psychological, dreams themselves are psychological even if the mechanisms of dreaming are not. Although there are some connections between REM sleep and near-death experiences, and REM sleep can even

32 Kondziella et al., "Migraine Aura," 13–14.

33. Kondziella et al., "Migraine Aura," 15.

intrude into an individual's waking life,[34] some people will actively choose to engage in an imaginative fantasy life. A 2018 study was focused on whether such an active fantasy life can affect whether that individual will have a near-death experience.[35]

Fantasy proneness has been researched in the past, and it was this past research that was used to define the terms and guide the process of this study. Fantasy proneness can be as simple as day-dreaming or as as complex as hallucinations that are indiscernible from reality. People prone to fantasies also tend to report more paranormal and more intense religious experiences. There were two common but divergent themes that ran among those with fantasy proneness: first, they may have grown up in a situation in which their parents encouraged engaging in such behavior; second, they may have used it as a coping mechanism for negative childhood experiences, which seems to have occurred more frequently with such individuals.[36]

In another study used by the researchers, it was noted that those with fantasy proneness were not any more likely to have false memories than those who were not prone to fantasies.[37] This is even though those with proneness to fantasy would usually self-report more vivid imagery than those without it. Interestingly, external be-havioral testing of participants for the vividness of imagery showed no difference between those prone to fantasy and those who were not.[38] All this seems to suggest that fantasy proneness has less to do with the cognitive process and has more to do with the personali-ties of those who report high fantasy proneness.

Those being examined in the 2018 study included people who reported having the symptoms of a near-death experience and suf-ficiently met the definition. Over 40% met the criteria of a near-death experience even though they were not in a life-threatening situation. A third group consisted of those who have never had a

34. Kondziella, Dreier, and Olsen, "Prevalence of Near-Death," 1.

35. Martial et al., "Fantasy Proneness Correlates," 1.

36. Merckelbach, Horselenberg, and Muris, "Creative Experiences," 988.

37 Aleman and Haan, "Fantasy Proneness," 1751.

38 Aleman and Haan, "Fantasy Proneness," 1751.

near-death experience nor have been in a life-threatening situation. The control group consisted of one hundred individuals, with half reporting a life-threatening situation but no near-death experience and the other half reporting no known life-threatening situation.

In gauging whether an individual was prone to fantasies, the researchers avoided asking the question outright. Rather, they asked questions regarding specific fantasy-related questions to determine a proneness for fantasies. The questions were set up as true or false, allowing the researchers to create a score based on the sum of the responses. This score was then compared to the experience score of their near-death experiences.

The researchers found no significant difference among the age groups of participants, nor did they find a significant difference in the intensity of near-death experiences between those who had them in life-threatening circumstances and those who claimed to have them in non-life-threatening circumstances. Because of the nature of the control group, the researchers had no data to report for it in this circumstance.[39]

There was, however, still a significant difference between the groups. Those who had a near-death experience in non-life-threatening situations also had high levels of fantasy proneness in comparison to all other groups in the study. Those who had near-death experiences with life-threatening circumstances and the control group did not have a significant difference between them. Between the control group and those with neither near-death experiences nor life-threatening experiences, there was no difference at all. For all those (at the individual level) who reported having a near-death experience, a positive correlation existed between their near-death experience score and the score of their fantasy proneness.[40]

Although the researchers could not make any conclusions on the data, they were able to hypothesize that those who had high levels of fantasy proneness were more likely to report subjective and nonlife-threatening near-death experiences because of that proneness when exposed to the right conditions. Because those

39. Martial et al., "Fantasy Proneness Correlates," 3.
40. Martial et al., "Fantasy Proneness Correlates," 4.

who reported a "classical" near-death experience (those who have scored highly on measuring for a genuine near-death experience while in a life-threatening situation) did not correlate with their fantasy-proneness, the researchers could not conclude that this proneness affected near-death experiences in general.[41]

While the intensity of the near-death experiences did not seem to differ between those who were in life-threatening experiences and those who were not, those who did not report a life-threatening situation had a correlation between the intensity of their near-experiences and the levels of fantasy-proneness. The researchers made clear, however, that correlation does not equate to causality and there should be more research done in areas of neurology in relation to near-death experiences. They also maintained that there should be further research into the relationship between fantasy-proneness and having an experience like a near-death experience as there may be a correlation to this personality trait, and the "extreme internal focus in individuals could, in some cases, result in memories of subjective experiences meeting the identification criteria of NDEs but occurring without a life-threatening situation."[42]

The researchers acknowledge some of the shortcomings in their research. One problem they encountered was that the term itself, "Near-death Experience," has no universal definition, which creates difficulty in determining what events should be included. Because such events could include life-threatening situations and situations that are not, such as those under anesthesia, a better-defined definition would be beneficial to the research community as well as those who are struggling to define their experience. Furthermore, the personality trait of fantasy-proneness may have skewed the selection process as they may tend to be more likely to share their "non-ordinary experiences." There was also the issue of all medical information being self-reported, so any information on whether the reporting individual was or was not in a life-threatening situation was not medically verified.[43]

41. Martial et al., "Fantasy Proneness Correlates," 4.
42. Martial et al., "Fantasy Proneness Correlates," 4–5.
43. Martial et al., "Fantasy Proneness Correlates," 5–6.

The final issue was the overlap between the test for general fantasy proneness and the test for near-death experiences. The former "focuses on lifetime experiences" while the latter "focuses on one major event." However, even when removing those areas of potential overlap, there was still a strong correlation, as noted above. Although there was no clear answer for the researchers, they believed that more clinical research would be needed in the area of cognitive function.[44]

While fantasy proneness is something individuals may actively engage in, it is reasonable to ask whether mental illness plays a role in having a near-death experience. However, mental fitness appears to have no role in whether someone has a near-death experience.

There is also the possibility that reports of near-death experiences are fabricated to one extent or another. This does not necessitate lying or intentional deception; rather, there is the possibility of those with near-death experiences having false memories. Previous research indicates that there does not appear to be any correlation between false memories and fantasy proneness;[45] however, some of the same researchers from the previous study wanted to see if there was more to be said about false memories and near-death experiences. They "postulate[d] that NDEs could be built as a result of the individuals' attempt to interpret their highly stressful and confusing experiences to preserve a coherent interpretation of the events associated with episodes of altered consciousness."[46]

Much research has been done in the area of false memories, and the researchers applied much of this to specifically addressing near-death experiences. They were able to successfully plant false memories into the participants, including specific details that had not actually occurred. One of the cited studies used word association for this task: using words of a similar concept and then inserting a "critical" word that was not part of the original word list. Participants would not only believe that the false word to be part of the list but would have false memories of having seen it. The

---

44. Martial et al., "Fantasy Proneness Correlates," 6.

45 Haan, "Fantasy Proneness," 1751.

46 Martial et al., "False Memory Susceptibility," 807.

participants would usually also have a high level of confidence in these false memories.[47]

Such cases seem to be higher in those who believe they have recovered traumatic memories (which are in turn usually false) and in those who tend to dissociate, which the researchers define as "the detachment of thoughts, feelings, or experiences from the normal stream of consciousness and memory" and affects how people interpret experiences. Furthermore, people who have had a near-death experience seem to tend to have "high-dissociative traits" and it is believed that they are more likely to have false or distorted memories.[48]

In fact, one of the cited studies indicated that false memories may be believed to be more real than actual memories of events that happened. Imagined events that contained a lot of information (but were easy to recall) were far more likely to be perceived as real than those that did not have much information. The study also showed that false memories had more to do with disassociation than with suggestibility.[49]

The question is then whether those with near-death experiences are indeed more susceptible to having false memories. They predicted that the participants who reported having near-death experiences would be more likely than the control group of participants to falsely recall the critical lures. They also predicted that those with near-death experiences would also have more details surrounding the false memories.

The researchers surveyed twenty people who reported having a near-death experience and a control group of twenty volunteers who had been in life-threatening situations but without having had a near-death experience. All participants were French speakers recruited online and in local publications. There was no financial incentive, and all volunteers were screened for memory impairment as well neurological and mental disorders.[50]

---

47. Roediger and McDermott, "Creating False Memories," 809.

48. Martial et al., "False Memory Susceptibility," 807–808.

49 Heaps and Nash, "Individual Differences," 313, 316–17.

50 Martial et al., "False Memory Susceptibility," 808–809.

The researchers had a recorded voice read lists of words to the participants. They were then instructed to write down as many of the words that they could remember hearing from the list (with a small task to be done between hearing the words and recalling them). They were then asked to indicate whether they specifically remembered the word, if they knew whether the word was part of the list without a specific memory of it, or if they merely guessed the word. Lastly, they were given a final test in which they were asked if there were any words that they did not include but which they may have recalled because they had no specific memory of the word coming up on the list.[51]

The first thing the researchers found was a low rate of guessing across both groups. The second thing they found was that both groups were equally confident in what they correctly recalled. However, the groups diverged when it came to false recollections. Both groups had the same level of false recollections, but the near-death experience group was far more confident in the false recollections, including recalling specific details surrounding their occurrence. In the meantime, these same false recollections were more likely to be labeled a guess by the non-near-death experience group.

The researchers believed that the reason that those with near-death experiences describe them as being more real than reality is that they are more prone to having "illusory recollection"[52] such as remembering vivid details of an event that did not actually happen. The individual's background beliefs and experiences can cause them to attempt to find a way to interpret their experience, and their "cognitive processing style might then lead to a highly subjective and very detailed episodic representation of the event."[53]

When it came to the critical lure, both groups were equally likely to recall it during the initial recall test, but during the post-recall, the near-death experience group was less likely to recall a critical lure. The greatest difference between the groups came from those who had near-death experiences believing that they were

51. Martial et al., "False Memory Susceptibility," 809–10.
52. Martial et al., "False Memory Susceptibility," 813.
53. Martial et al., "False Memory Susceptibility," 814.

remembering the critical lure rather than believing it came from their own thoughts. The researchers believe that the implication of this is that it is possible to have near-death experiences but recognize them as being something "internally generated" rather than having been an actual experience. They acknowledge that further research would be needed in this area.[54]

THEOLOGICAL

Exploration of near-death experiences have not been restricted to the realms of biology or psychology. Although this book examines the value of near-death experiences in Christian apologetics (as demonstrated by the way Gary Habermas has used it in his works), there are a variety of ways that these experiences have been interpreted theologically. In various other religions, there are accounts of near-death experiences, and they seem to be quite similar to those in the West, although with their own unique, cultural perspective.

Deepak Chopra recounts a story of a young woman who initially put herself in a near-death state while sick, knowing full well that she may not be able to return to the living. Over the course of five days, she saw Buddhist versions of Heaven and Hell, saw what happened to the righteous and evildoers alike, and even interacted with the god of death. He, knowing she would return to her body, gave her messages to pass on to the living. Upon returning to her body, she was able to reveal things about the living and the dead alike, things she had no prior way of knowing.[55]

A study conducted in Iran within an Islamic context showed that the generalities of near-death experiences were much the same, with experiences such as bliss, out-of-body experiences, or seeing what they believed to be something beyond the natural realm. According to the researchers, Iranian Muslims tend to be more fearful of death and consider it a taboo. Despite this, those who had such an experience seemed to lose this sense of fear.[56]

---

54 Martial et al., "False Memory Susceptibility," 814.

55. Chopra, *Life After Death*, 37–38.

56 Khoshab et al., "Near-Death Experience," 417.

Another study conducted in Sri Lanka compared near-death experiences across the variety of religious groups at a hospital. These groups were Buddhist, Hindu, Muslim, and Christian, with Buddhism (which they called a nontheistic religion) being the most prevalent. They found that the three theist groups had significantly more near-death experiences than the Buddhist group.[57] The researchers pointed out that Christians (the second largest group studied) have concrete beliefs about the afterlife, whereas the views of the afterlife held by the Buddhists were more fluid. They believed this to be an area requiring further specific study.[58]

When it comes to Christianity, belief in returning from the dead is certainly not unknown. Aside from Jesus' own Resurrection, the Bible relates a variety of people who return from death. In John 11, Jesus raises Lazarus from the grave after being dead for three days. Acts 9 recounts an event in which a young woman got sick and died, and after the household had prepared her for burial Peter comes and raises her from the dead. This is by no means an exhaustive list, but it establishes that Christians believe that returning from a state of death is possible, for as Mark 9:23 states, "All things are possible for one who believes." It is important to note, however, that there is no biblical record of what any of these individuals saw or experienced during their state of death.

SUMMARY

Although a common theme across all these studies is that more research is needed, the pieces of the puzzle that is near-death experiences also seem to be coming together to form a coherent explanation (or explanations) for what is happening to the individual. Common biological, psychological, and theological themes appear to come up across the research. The naturalist seems to be gaining the advantage in the discussion over the implications of the afterlife that near-death experiences have to offer.

57. Chandradasa et al., "Near-Death Experiences," 1602.
58. Chandradasa et al., "Near-Death Experiences," 1603–1604.

For Gary Habermas, however, most of these reported cases of near-death experiences are of little concern. Instead, Habermas prefers to focus on "the many well-documented reports of individuals who have provided accurate descriptions of their surroundings while they were in a near-death state," and in some cases may have described a setting or events that occurred miles away.[59] What, in a naturalist worldview, could account for such occurrences? If verified, such claims would certainly be a crushing blow to the honest naturalist, even if all other characteristics of near-death experiences (such as encountering heavenly beings or embarking upon a spiritual journey[60]) could be accounted for. For the Christian apologist, it is crucial that such events could be verified in order to use them in his apologetics.

59. Habermas, *Risen Jesus and Future Hope*, 60.
60 Long, "Near-Death Experience," 372.

3

The Claims of Gary Habermas

THE PRIMARY CHRISTIAN APPROACH to near-death experiences that will be examined will be that of Gary Habermas. Habermas is a Distinguished Research Professor for Liberty University who specializes in the Resurrection of Jesus. His expertise in this area has led him to work at fifteen graduate seminaries. Within many of his works on the Resurrection, he has included apologetic work on near-death experiences, and it is these sources that will follow. Before examining his work, however, there must first be a discussion on evidence and how to determine whether it is of value.

A BRIEF PRIMER ON EVIDENCE
FOR THE MIRACULOUS

Gary Habermas believes that most claims surrounding near-death experiences are not helpful to the Christian making his case against the naturalist. He puts little stock in the apologetic value of those attributes that are most central to the near-death experience. Rather, he focuses on those few reports that he believes contain events that can truly be corroborated. Reports of people who were able to describe things that happened in the room or several miles away, and in some cases, blind people accurately describing things they could perceive visually while in a state of near-death.[1]

1. Habermas and Licona, *Case for Resurrection of Jesus*, 146.

Such claims are, however, quite extraordinary. It seems appropriate to turn to the words of Carl Sagan when it comes to such extraordinary claims. In the television series *Cosmos*, examining claims made by those who argue for the possibility of extraterrestrial life having arrived on earth at some point in the past, Sagan set his standard: "What counts is not what sounds plausible, not what we'd like to believe, not what one or two witnesses claim, but only what is supported by hard evidence, rigorously and skeptically examined. Extraordinary claims require extraordinary evidence."[2]

This sentiment is not merely a refrain for many naturalists, it is considered by some to be foundational to scientific skepticism.[3] Although Habermas's (and any other claimant's) assertions should not be given a free pass merely because it seems to agree with a favored position, Sagan's hard line on the types of evidence that are acceptable may go too far.

David Deming believes that when Sagan spoke his infamous words, he failed to define what he meant by extraordinary—both in terms of claims and what would constitute appropriate evidence. Even if one is to distinguish between things that are beyond nature and those things which are simply beyond our current scientific understanding, a problem arises: how to know into which category a phenomenon falls, because even an apparently supernatural event may simply be a natural event. This event may be one that is currently not fully understood by the scientific community.[4]

Furthermore, there is the issue of being able to define what precisely would constitute "extraordinary evidence." This idea, though an incredibly popular one, is impossible to quantify or use as an objective standard. It is instead a sort of "social agreement" among scientists, even if it is ill-defined.[5]

For Deming, the solution is clear: properly define what is meant by "extraordinary," and he believes that the best way to define it is the same way David Hume did, which is that a claim can

2. Sagan, "Encyclopaedia Galactica."
3. Voss, Helgen and Jansa, "Extraordinary Claims," 893.
4 Deming, "Extraordinary Claims," 1320–21.
5 Tressoldi, "Extraordinary Claims," 1.

be rejected if there is a large amount of evidence that contradicts it. There can be things that have never been observed that may be true or false but cannot be rejected outright if there is no evidence to the contrary. This allows a naturalist the ability to reject supernatural events (such as miracles) while allowing for new scientific discoveries that may go beyond what is currently known about the laws of nature.[6]

Although it may seem like little more than punting the question posed above further down the road, it is fair to ask whether Hume's standard is appropriate to use in examining the evidence presented by Habermas. According to Hume, the only way a claim can be true (or at least one that can be justified in believing) is if there is evidence equal to or greater than what is believed. All of humanity has seen people die, all of humanity has seen heavy objects fall to the ground, and all of humanity has seen fire burn away wood. Because there is so much (literally, a world of) evidence that these things occur, then any claim to the contrary must be rejected outright, no matter who is making the claim.[7]

Hume's claim extends even beyond this. He seems to suggest that even if there was absolute proof of a miraculous event, the fact that all previous historical evidence goes against the possibility of the event in question is therefore not a miracle. Indeed, all of humanity would have to agree on the event occurring for there to be any acceptance of the fact.

If all nations across the globe reported a single event (in his example, a week of utter darkness), then perhaps the event becomes far less doubtful, even if Hume still retains a bit of doubt. On the other hand, if all the physicians in England claimed that the Queen had truly passed away and she was seen a month later by the entire royal court, this would not be enough evidence for Hume to accept the claim. Instead, he would believe them to be lying.[8]

Following this train of thought could lead one to readily reject all claims of the miraculous, particularly that of the early apostles

---

6. Deming, "Extraordinary Claims," 1329.

7 Hume, "Of Miracles," 33.

8. Hume, "Of Miracles," 41–43.

in proclaiming a resurrected Jesus Christ. In 1 Corinthians 15, the Apostle Paul wrote that the risen Jesus had appeared to all twelve Disciples, along with a few specific other people. Among them, he states that there Jesus appeared to an additional five hundred people. Paul does not mention them merely to make his number of eyewitnesses sound more credible. Instead, he mentions these five hundred along with the fact that most of them are still alive. His purpose in mentioning that specific detail is to set up the possibility for doubters to question living eyewitnesses to see if their accounts matched up with what Paul was saying.[9]

If a Humian approach would lead someone to reject the witness of over five hundred people, it would certainly lead him to reject Paul's own claim that he had seen the risen Jesus. This, even though Paul went beyond being a mere skeptic to being an actual persecutor of the Christian faith. One would also reject the basis for his understanding of the Gospel account that he most likely received from the Apostle Peter.[10]

Is Hume's claim that it is only reasonable to accept a miracle if the number of witnesses was not one, or twelve, or even five hundred? What if the number was two thousand? What if that number was between fifty and a hundred thousand? The famous Fatima miracles provide such an example. These miracles began as visions of the Virgin Mary described by three shepherd children in Portugal, a country whose Christian faith (which was overwhelmingly of the Catholic denomination) was on the verge of extinction.[11] As word of their visions spread, between two and three thousand people showed up to see for themselves, and they witnessed the children have a vision. One could attribute this to the children being particularly good actors and the crowd was one that was ready

9 Craig, *On Guard*, 232–33.

10 Habermas, *Risen Jesus and Future Hope*, 18–20.

11. Protestants may object to the use of a Catholic miracle, but by the eyewitness standard that was used above this miracle should be taken into consideration, although a thorough discussion of what happened at Fatima is outside the scope of this book. The Christology of Catholics is the same as of Protestants.

to be convinced, but it is the final event at Fatima that points to something truly miraculous.

The day and time of this event were predicted well ahead of time. On the day of the miracle, it rained the entire morning, letting up as the miracle needed to occur. The event was witnessed by over fifty thousand people and possibly as many as one hundred thousand. Most of those who were there agreed that the sun acted in an erratic fashion, which they watched without any eye injury. Their clothes, wet from a day of rain, were reported to dry almost instantly. Portugal's Catholic heritage experienced a huge revival.[12]

Would Hume allow for such a testimony? Most likely not. If all the doctors in England would be assumed to be liars if they claimed a miracle,[13] then it is doubtful that he could be convinced by the resurrection of anyone at all, let alone that of a first-century Jew with no truly significant following until well after his death (as suggested in Luke 16:31). Hume may not accept it, and naturalists like Deming may wish to use Hume as his ultimate standard of determining the truth,[14] but it needs to be asked if someone's opinion, even if that individual's word carries a lot of academic weight, is enough to determine what counts as reality and what does not. Perhaps it is true that "The cosmos is all that is, or was, or ever will be,"[15] but Hume and those who follow must still substantiate this claim beyond merely disagreeing with the alternative.

Rejecting all evidence of miracles simply because most of human history shows that the opposite is consistently true would make it necessary to reject any highly improbable event simply because the opposite is almost always more consistently true. William Lane Craig uses the example of a lottery to make this point. If a newspaper reported the previous night's winning lottery ticket number, the probability of that number having been pulled is highly improbable. Because it is so highly improbable that the specific lottery number would be pulled, reports of the winning lottery number must be

---

12 McNabb and Blado, "Mary and Fátima," 58–59.

13 Hume, "Of Miracles," 41–43.

14. Deming, "Extraordinary Claims," 1329.

15 Sagan, "Shores of the Cosmic Ocean."

rejected. The only way Hume's standard could be met is if there is evidence of the newspaper's reliability that can meet or exceed the improbability of the winning lottery number being pulled.[16]

Richard Purtill also mounts a defense against a Humean approach, further illustrating why that approach to evidence regarding an extraordinary claim falls short. Purtill points out that Hume is mistaken about whether something should meet the uniform experience of humanity, because even holding to the laws of nature, there may be events that are unknown or have never occurred before but still fall within those laws. He points out that Hume uses the example of a healthy man suddenly dying, to contrast it with a miracle (specifically, the Resurrection), as being a very rare event but occurring frequently enough that it can be accepted as fact. Purtill suggests that this line of reasoning would not allow him to distinguish between a miracle and a very unusual yet plausible event.[17]

Finally, Norman Geisler's response should be enough to fully reject a Humean approach to evidence Habermas has to offer, let alone any demands for extraordinary evidence. Geisler first points out that in order to claim any specific experience as being uniform one would have to know whether it truly is a uniform experience and to read claims across history there are many that are claims of miracles. Hume also seems to make the mistake of valuing the quantity of evidence over the quality of evidence.

Science then becomes little more than a democratic vote on truth because, no matter how great the evidence is for a true resurrection, the fact will always remain that more people stay dead than are resurrected (and with one notable exception, those who are resurrected also eventually die as well). Geisler warns, "Rational belief should not . . . be determined by majority vote."[18] Perhaps more astoundingly, a Humean approach would force everyone to outright reject a miraculous event, even if it was in every way authentic and

16 Craig, *Reasonable Faith*, 270.

17. Purtill, "Defining Miracles," 65–66.

18 Geisler, "Miracle and the Modern Mind," 78–79.

verifiable, which a rational person should accept even if uniformity of experience existed across history.[19]

Geisler shows further inconsistencies with a Humian approach. Patterns used to establish laws of nature would not allow for new laws of nature to be discovered or for current laws to be adjusted. Geisler offers the example of Newtonian physics being the law of nature regarding the laws of motion and the theory of relativity being formulated to describe and account for the exceptions to Newtonian physics. Using a Humean approach would force one to reject that the exceptions ever occurred.

Finally, Geisler shows that the basis of what is known may typically be through what is repeatedly experienced in the past, but that should be held separate from the event that is being examined. Modern scientists point to the universe coming from the Big Bang at the beginning of time, but this is a single event—unrepeated and unrepeatable. This event, Geisler argues, is itself a miracle. Using this sort of principle, Geisler argues that rather than disprove the possibility of miracles, Hume managed to provide a reliable method to determine when something miraculous has occurred.[20]

Various attempts to modernize Hume's arguments have been attempted, arguably most effectively from Anthony Flew. Although most naturalists seem to focus on Hume's argument specifically, therefore, there will not be much time spent looking at approaching the argument, Flew's work is worth a brief mention. Flew was quite influenced by Hume, writing that Hume "was also the first thinker of the modern period to develop systematically a world outlook that was thoroughly skeptical, this-worldly, and human-centered."[21]

Flew did, however, recognize some flaws in Hume's original argument and sought to defend what was strong and improve what was not.[22] As mentioned above, Hume's argument is the one most cited for our purposes, so time will not be spent discussing Flew's arguments and rebuttals. Then why, one might ask, bring up Flew

---

19. Geisler, "Miracle and the Modern Mind," 80.

20. Geisler, "Miracle and the Modern Mind," 81–82.

21 Flew, "Neo-Humean Arguments," 45.

22 Flew, "Neo-Humean Arguments," 49.

at all? Because Flew, an ardent defender of Hume and a renowned atheist philosopher, would eventually abandon his own naturalistic beliefs, rejecting his own arguments against theism. This was thanks in no small part to near-death experiences.[23]

As discussed above, Carl Sagan and David Hume's methodologies are both to be rejected as imprecise and impractical when dealing with the subject of the supernatural. What then should be expected from Gary Habermas's claims and the evidence for it? No need for them to be extraordinary or abundant, they must simply be of good quality. The quality of the evidence will determine the value of Habermas's claims.[24]

THE CLAIMS AND THEIR EVIDENCE

Almost all near-death experiences share certain characteristics, including out of body experiences, bright lights, positive feelings, flashbacks to various moments of their lives, and interactions with various spiritual beings and those they believe to be family members.[25] However, most of these events seem to have biological or psychological explanations. Although not much seems to be known for sure, there are many explanations that need a bit more research but seem promising for researchers.[26]

What evidence can Habermas provide that would readily suggest that even though the vast majority of near-death experiences can be explained by biological or psychological means, there could still be cases that provide a case for the supernatural? What sort of evidence could be provided that would convince even an atheist like Anthony Flew that there is a reality beyond the observable natural world around him? It is only these much rarer occurrences that Habermas uses.

The evidence that Habermas wishes to bring to the discussion is related to those who had no measurable heart or brain activity

23. Habermas, *Risen Jesus and Future Hope*, 61.

24 Hawkes, "Extraordinary Claims," 1935.

25. Moody, "Getting Comfortable with Death," 369.

26 Martial et al., "False Memory Susceptibility," 814.

but were able to report things from when they were dead that were corroborated, including those who are blind. Some of these scenarios involved the patient having no activity for hours at a time. Each of these cases involved actual events or surrounding details that could not have been known to the patient and could be corroborated later.[27] Although he recounts these events in various books, his argument seems to be best laid out in his book with J. P. Moreland, *Beyond Death: Exploring the Evidence of Immortality*.

Habermas and Moreland seem to rely on a variety of sources, but for the most part, they seem to be out of print and difficult to find. Fortunately, one source they seem to lean upon rather frequently is the 1990 book, *Closer to the Light: Learning from the Near-Death Experiences of Children*, written by Melvin Morse and Paul Perry, which he believes provides reasonable evidence of collaborated accounts of those with near-death experiences.[28]

One story involved a young girl, Katie, who was not expected to survive a night (and the only thing keeping her alive was machinery) made a full recovery within a few days. Morse, who was the doctor who oversaw her care, interviewed her and her parents upon recovery. She was able to describe the doctors she saw and what order they entered her room. She was also able to describe where she was taken and what physically occurred to her during that time, including the fact that she had a nasal rather than much more common oral intubation. Aside from the spiritual aspects (such as encountering spiritual beings) that she described, she was also able to describe what her parents and siblings were doing at home, as well as what clothing they had been wearing.

Morse questioned the parents on their religious beliefs to see if they may have influenced what Katie saw during her near-death experience. Her parents were nominal Mormons who regularly attended religious services with no beliefs about spiritual guides, although they did believe in an afterlife. Morse would confirm their beliefs with another doctor who was also a practicing Mormon.[29]

---

27. Habermas, *Risen Jesus and Future Hope*, 60–61.

28 Habermas and Moreland, *Beyond Death*, 157.

29. Morse and Perry, *Closer to the Light*, 3–8.

Habermas and Moreland follow this up with another account from Morse, which involves a young boy who not only had an out-of-body experience but was able to determine where he (in a spiritual sense) would go as his body was taken to the hospital, along with speeding ahead of his ambulance to reach the hospital.[30] The boy, Rick, claims to have seen the world through his sister's eyes by entering her body, seeing his father getting ready to leave the house, and watching the person who was removed from his room in the hospital to make space for him. From there, his account takes on a tone that is more typical near-death experience as he leaves earth and travels down a tunnel of light and has feelings of bliss. These stories were said to have "amazed" his family.[31]

Habermas and Moreland express their interest in near-death experiences involving blind people. Although they do not go into the details of any one case in their book, they mention a chemist who went blind but who was able to describe his surroundings. They also mention that there are various other reports of people who had been blind for years and yet who were able to describe visually what they had seen, and for verification they were tested for blindness after these experiences. "These cases," Habermas and Moreland insist, "are not rare; they are unexpectedly common."[32]

Once again, attention is turned to Morse's findings. Once again, an out-of-body experience seems to be a strong indicator of the near-death experience. A young boy was in the hospital without a heartbeat for twenty minutes, with the medical personnel believing his case was beyond the hope of resuscitation. He was eventually revived by receiving an electric shock via cardioversion paddle.

Some years later, he was interviewed by Morse. According to Morse, it took some probing for the young man to open up about his experience, but once he did, he described an out-of-body experience and reported being in the operating room, on the ceiling, while the doctors worked on him below. He described what the doctors did and what they said in the room, as well as the painful

30 Habermas and Moreland, *Beyond Death*, 158.
31 Morse and Perry, *Closer to the Light*, 177–78.
32. Habermas and Moreland, *Beyond Death*, 158.

sensation of getting the shock and returning to his body. Morse was impressed with the accuracy that he was able to describe the procedure, as well as noticing details about the room and about the medical personnel themselves.[33]

The list of cases that Habermas and Moreland describe go on much the same as those that have been discussed above. Although the details change in each case, the core elements stay approximately the same. These include descriptions of medical procedures and details of their rooms or of the medical personnel. Some of these details came through conversations that Habermas or Moreland had themselves with those involved. There is, however, one more line of evidence that they employ that they believe adds weight to their argument: those with near-death experiences seeing and interacting with deceased family members or friends that they did not know they had died.[34]

One such case involved a woman who was dying and began calling out the names of loved ones that she saw that had already passed away. She yelled out in surprise when she saw the face of her cousin whom she had thought to be alive. When she was resuscitated, she learned that her cousin had died a week prior. Another case involved a woman who had a near-death experience and believed that she saw Heaven and, while there, interacted with her friend Tom, who had just arrived there himself. A few hours after returning to her body, she was informed that Tom had died in an automobile accident. In several different accounts, the individual who died was not even aware of the family member's existence yet claim to have interacted with that family member.[35]

One such account is from an eyewitness, Maurice Rawlings, who watched a man collapse from a heart attack right in front of him while hooked up to an EKG. While resuscitating the man, Rawlings claims that the man would come to and beg him to continue bringing him back because each time Rawlings stopped or slowed down the man would slip into what he believed was Hell. Upon full

---

33 Morse and Perry, *Closer to the Light*, 27–30.

34. Habermas and Moreland, *Beyond Death*, 159–61.

35 Habermas and Moreland, *Beyond Death*, 162–63.

resuscitation, the man became a Christian within moments of his experience. He would later report one episode of slipping away in which he met his mother in a beautiful place, whom he had never met and had no idea what she looked like. He was then able to identify his mother in a picture out of a crowd of women.[36]

Habermas and Moreland seem to believe that the corroboration methods used by those cited are reliable. One such researcher, Michael Sabom, would gather a group of people who had previous heart attack experiences and of similar demographics as those with near-death experiences. He checked to see if they would remember the details of caring for a heart attack patient, whether through their direct experience in the hospital or from what they had gleaned from medical television and movies. When surveyed, even those who were able to describe the process most accurately did not get nearly as many details correct as those who claimed to have witnessed the procedure via their own near-death experiences.[37]

Morse used a couple of methods in his research, including having a control group and ruling out the effects of any hallucinogenic drugs or sleep deprivation which the control group, as well as the studied group, may have been under. He took steps to eliminate anyone who may have invented a narrative to be included in the research. His research was well-received by the academic community, and he noted that their near-death experiences may very well be a natural part of the process of death.[38]

SUMMARY

"Extraordinary claims require extraordinary evidence," Carl Sagan famously declared,[39] and Gary Habermas's claims are certainly extraordinary. What sort of evidence should be used in determining the effectiveness of what Habermas has to say? Does it truly need to be "extraordinary"?

36. Rawlings, *Beyond Death's Door*, 2–5.
37 Habermas and Moreland, *Beyond Death*, 165.
38 Morse and Perry, *Closer to the Light*, 21–23, 47–49.
39 Sagan, "Encyclopaedia Galactica," 1:12.

As discussed above, the evidence need not be exceptional or extraordinary, it must simply be of sufficient quality to support the claim.[40] The imprecise language of the term, "extraordinary," will lead to confusion, and even outright rejection of perfectly valid claims and arguments simply because the evidence may not be as grand as it is expected to be.[41] So, have the claims of Gary Habermas been presented with evidence of sufficient quality to allow the Christian to use near-death experiences in making his case for theism?

40. Hawkes, "Extraordinary Claims," 1935.
41 Deming, "Do Extraordinary Claims," 1320.

4

Evaluating Habermas's Claims

MOST OF THE COMMON traits of near-death experiences appear
to be explained or approaching explanation. However, it was not
the cases that involved these common traits that were the focus of
Habermas's use of near-death experiences in making his case for
Christianity. For Habermas, the focus needed to be on those near-
death experiences where the individual could report something
that was able to be verified by the family or the medical personnel
involved in the incident. The other common characteristics, though
quintessential of near-death experiences, would do little to prove
anything against naturalism.[1]

THE NATURE OF THE CLAIMS

Essentially all of Habermas's examples involve out-of-body experiences in which the individual saw things from on high, whether
next to their body or from a distance. These include accounts of
people who were without brain or heart activity for extended periods of time, and in some cases, of blind individuals. Habermas
also cites some others who studied near-death experiences and described cases in which patients were able to describe corroborated
details and events.

1. Habermas, *Risen Jesus and Future Hope*, 60.

In many of these cases, the claims are assured to be corroborated, though it is not always clear who corroborated what event.[2] In the case of Melvin Morse's Katie, her ability to repeat what occurred and what medical procedures were used were verified in private interviews with Morse, with events from her accompanying out of body experience being confirmed by her parents. For an understanding of why Katie had the sort of near-death experiences that she did, Morse's go-to place for where she must have gotten her ideas about the afterlife, guardian angels, and tunnels of light is her parents' religious beliefs, which he verifies with another Mormon doctor he works with. Curiously absent from his investigation were the books or cartoons that may have influenced her. In the case of Rick, as documented by Morse, the only people who were able to verify anything Rick claims to have seen are his immediate family members.[3]

In fact, a large portion of Morse's research is interviewing those who had their experiences as children and were recounting those experiences as adults. He admits that this sort of evidence is purely anecdotal but believes that such evidence is still scientifically valid.[4] Citing both breastfeeding, fluoridation of drinking water, and the use of aspirin in preventing heart attacks, he points to the fact that much scientific advancement has come from such anecdotal evidence. In each of these examples, the anecdotal evidence was eventually followed up by scientific research and verified.

Morse got a variety of people from all walks of life together for his interviews, with the only real stipulations being that they had a near-death experience and were mentally healthy and not drug users. Morse also had help from another researcher who would do the same study with a different group of patients. This would be done separately from Morse's work to see whether the results would be the same or similar or whether there would be large differences. When it was all concluded, the accounts were all very similar. At the

---

2 Habermas, *Risen Jesus and Future Hope*, 60–61.

3. Morse and Perry, *Closer to the Light*, 5–8, 177–78.

4. Morse and Perry, *Closer to the Light*, 164.

end of it all, however, they were simply accounts told by those who had near-death experiences.[5]

PREEMPTING SOME OBJECTIONS

Habermas, together with Moreland, preempts some of the objections one may have against near-death experiences as being valid evidence for the existence of an afterlife or a soul. The objections fall broadly into two categories: worldview issues and medical objections. These questions are then addressed before moving on to more contemporary issues in discussing near-death experiences. For the purposes of more fully exploring the claims and their objections (along with rebuttals to the objections), the defense of events that supposedly have been corroborated will be grouped into a third category and the most immediately relevant points will be examined.

Objections Based on Worldview

There are some possible objections to the use of near-death experiences that involve the Christian worldview. How does a Christian reconcile what the individual experiences with what Christianity teaches? A worldview is the way any given individual will understand the world around them and interpret the experiences he has.[6] Although it appears that backgrounds that stem from worldviews (such as religious beliefs and country of origin) do not appear to affect whether someone has a near-death experience or whether they experience the common characteristics of a near-death experience,[7] there seems to be a wide range of ways people interpret these experiences.[8] As Douglas Groothuis points out, "The inquiring mind needs satisfy answers, not merely experiences."[9]

5 Morse and Perry, *Closer to the Light*, 164–67.

6. Groothuis, *Christian Apologetics*, 21.

7 Long, "Near-Death Experience," 372.

8. Habermas and Moreland, *Beyond Death*, 179.

9. Groothuis, *Christian Apologetics*, 20.

This leads to the first worldview objection: why do people who are Christians or from western countries identify the spiritual beings they encounter as angels or as Jesus while those from other backgrounds believe they interacted with their own major religious figures? Habermas and Moreland offer Westerners and Indians as an example.

While Westerners tend to see deceased loved ones or Christian religious figures, those from India tend to see Hindu religious figures such as Shiva or Krishna. Regarding these attitudes, Habermas and Moreland argue that the fact that various individuals have different perceptions of a common event does not mean that the event did not occur (as they point out from an article by William Wainwright).[10]

According to Wainwright, how a cognitive experience is interpreted is irrelevant to whether the experience occurred. Seeing various opposing religious figures does not invalidate the experience itself. In his example, seeing someone's personal belonging and believing that it belongs to someone else does not invalidate seeing the object, even if the interpretation of it is incorrect. This can even apply if several people see it and come to a different conclusion of whom it belongs to. It is worth noting that Wainwright seems to imply that a reasonable conclusion would be that *all* religions contain an understanding of the truth and are not contradictory at all.[11]

For Habermas and Moreland, this does not matter much in light of the fact that an experience occurred—never mind how it is interpreted by the individual because interpretations can be wrong. What really matters is that there was a neutral event: the near-death experience. This event should be considered neutral because it is "incapable of judging the truth or falsity of religious worldviews."[12]

Most people who describe near-death experiences say that it was an experience that was peaceful and full of bliss, and less than a quarter of those who report these experiences report them as being

10. Habermas and Moreland, *Beyond Death*, 179.

11. Wainwright, *Mysticism*, 107–10.

12. Habermas and Moreland, *Beyond Death*, 180.

negative.[13] This leads to the question, however, of why more people do not have a negative near-death experience or why there are no reports of people experiencing a judgement from God.[14] The Bible says in Hebrews 9:27, "It is appointed for every man to die once, and after that comes judgment." From the Christian perspective, it feels like there should be far more reports that are negative, and even positive experiences should involve a sense of judgement of some kind.

Habermas and Moreland turn again to Maurice Rawlings. After having resuscitated a man who claimed to have been in Hell while undergoing a near-death experience, Rawlings himself was so convinced he became a Christian as a result. However, when he spoke to the same man a few days later, the man had denied having had a hellish experience although he soon became a Christian as well. Rawlings believed this was because he suppressed the unbearable memories into his subconscious. He believes this is also why the reports tend to be so heavily positive: unless the patient is interviewed immediately the negative aspects of his experience will be shoved into the subconscious and "obliterated from recall."[15]

In response to Rawlings, Kenneth Ring acknowledge the existence of negative near-death experiences, but he found Rawlings' methodology to be flawed and his conclusions too greatly influenced by his Christian beliefs. Ring argued that negative (what he called "inverse") near-death experiences can be induced by various drugs. He, therefore, hypothesized that further research would show a higher number of patients to have had anesthesia at the time of their experience but would also show that these same patients did not receive enough anesthesia to fully block the painful physical experience.[16]

When it comes to the biblical text of Hebrews 9:27, cited above, Habermas and Moreland believed the most appropriate response comes down to biological death. They ask why the text should apply

13   Cook, et al., "What Happens," 27:05.

14   Habermas and Moreland, *Beyond Death*, 180.

15   Rawlings, *Beyond Death's Door*, 4–6.

16.   Ring, "Solving the Riddle," 6, 19–21.

to anything less than complete biological death, and why, if they are not completely dead, should anyone have a Hellish experience?[17] These questions seem to be a bit of a two-edged sword. To the latter question, the naturalist could simply respond by asking why anyone should have a Heavenly experience. As to the former question, it seems to try to rationalize why the biblical passage would not be relevant to near-death experiences while still trying to maintain the spiritual validity of those experiences.

The topic of interpretation comes into play again for Habermas and Moreland. Because every-day experiences that are common to almost everyone are already subject to a variety of interpretations, how much harder would it be for any individual to accurately interpret their near-death experience? Therefore, interpretations should be expected to vary.[18] For example, the conceptions of Heaven and Hell were far more complicated, and near-death experiences reflected this complexity.

In the modern world, beliefs about Heaven have been greatly simplified, and that too is reflected in the way people report their near-death experiences today.[19] In light of this, Habermas and Moreland believe that any specific interpretation of the afterlife should be discarded.[20]

Medical Objections

Perhaps the most immediately obvious question is what effect drugs may have on near-death experiences. Melvin Morse, in his study of near-death experiences involving twelve survivors of imminent death and a control group of 121 children who were ill but not near death, showed there is no connection between drugs (or lack of oxygen) and having a near-death experience. At the same time, all the 121 who were not near death were treated with various drugs

17 Habermas and Moreland, *Beyond Death*, 181.

18 Habermas and Moreland, *Beyond Death*,

19. Zaleski, *Otherworld Journeys*, 60.

20 Habermas and Moreland, *Beyond Death*, 181–82.

that are known to cause hallucinations. None of those 121 children in the control group had anything like a near-death experience.[21]

Because of Morse's work as well as the results of a few other studies, Habermas and Moreland reject the idea that drugs are the cause of near-death experiences, especially since hallucinations from medically administered drugs are nothing like that of near-death experiences.[22] As mentioned above, it is reasonable to hypothesize that in at least negative experiences drugs may play an active role (and ironically, it may be due to an inadequate amount of anesthesia).[23] Nevertheless, even if this is the case, such examples only account for a relatively small number of reported near-death experiences. According to Habermas and Moreland, those who have near-death experiences "have objectively perceived something beyond themselves."[24]

They also reject most underlying psychological issues or experiences as being a cause of near-death experiences. Citing a book published in 1977 (as well as the research done by Morse), they suggested that psychological effects and near-death experiences are not similar and in fact produce results contrary to each other.[25] As discussed above, more recent research indicates that psychology seems to play an active role in whether someone has a near-death experience, such as those who have an active fantasy life being more susceptible to near-death experiences[26] or the possibility of them being a false memory generated after the fact than being based on something that was actually experienced.[27] However, they again allow themselves a bit of an "out:" even if psychological conditions can account for various aspects of a near-death experience, it would not follow that the aspects of a near-death experience are explained,

---

21 Morse and Perry, *Closer to the Light*, 47–48.

22 Habermas and Moreland, *Beyond Death*, 184–85.

23 Ring, "Solving the Riddle," 20–21.

24. Habermas and Moreland, *Beyond Death*, 185.

25 Habermas and Moreland, *Beyond Death*, 186.

26 Martial et al., "Fantasy Proneness Correlates," 4–5.

27 Martial et al., "False Memory," 814.

nor would this account for things which they believe have been objectively verified.

They believe one of the tougher objections to near-death experiences as a supernatural phenomenon is the possibility that even in a near-death state, the individuals may have been able to see or hear more than previously thought possible. Although they seem to grant that this is a reasonable explanation for much of what could be thought of as an out-of-body near-death experience, they believe those that relate to a further distance disprove the idea, or at least do not lend it much weight.[28]

In the example of Katie, she was able to give details about her family's whereabouts and actions while she was miles away at the hospital, as verified by her family. There is also the example of Rick, who was able to describe various details of what occurred at his family's home as he was being cared for at the hospital.[29]

Habermas and Moreland also address the issue of accuracy and potential embellishment of reports. They believe that the best way to limit potential embellishment is by having the post-experience interview as soon as possible, although, in most cases, it appears that time between the near-death experience and the report seems to have little to no impact on accuracy. Considering the number of studies and the care taken by the researchers, they believe that this sort of research is similar to historical research.

They also bring up the objection of near-death experiences being fabrications. This, they feel, is the weakest of all the objections that have been brought up. They point out the fact that in general those who have had near-death experiences have nothing to gain by embellishing or fabricating their accounts. In some cases, they are not even aware of the questioner's intentions when they describe their experiences. Finally, the sheer amount of people who consistently report the same events should prevent most cases of fabrication.[30]

---

28. Habermas and Moreland, *Beyond Death*, 187.

29 Morse and Perry, *Closer to the Light*, 3–6, 177–178.

30 Habermas and Moreland, *Beyond Death*, 189–91.

Other Objections

Turning from broad objections to examining two specific perspectives, Habermas and Moreland addressed a detailed objection from a Christian and a detailed objection from a naturalist. Because the perspectives are radically different in worldview but both object to the existence of near-death experiences, Habermas and Moreland are able to address a wide range of specific objections, more so than in the broader categories.

Objections from a Christian Perspective

They begin with the perspective of H. Leon Greene, who is a cardiologist with a prestigious medical background, implying that he will be able to provide the very best objections from both a Christian as well as medical perspective.[31] Greene seems to reject near-death experiences as being valid, offering a variety of things that may account for them. These include fabrication, self-delusion, vivid imaginations, mass hysteria, or even demonic influences (although in this case, demonic influence would still be an action of the supernatural, arguably helping Habermas's larger point). Most likely, Greene believes, near-death experiences are a result of the brain attempting to make sense of what is physically occurring while gleaning from background experiences such as religious beliefs or what information the individual has from popular media accounts.[32]

Habermas and Moreland pointed out that aside from the medical arguments that Green made in his book, he makes theological and biblical issues a core part of his argument. Although they strongly imply that they believe these arguments are "tangential" to the debate at hand, they believe these arguments need to be addressed and corrected. This seems to tie in with what they believe to be philosophical errors on Greene's part.

Biblically, Greene's literal interpretation of John's description of Jesus in his apocalyptic vision seems to be a source of unnecessary

31. Habermas and Moreland, *Beyond Death*, 199–200.

32. Greene, *If I Should Wake*, 114.

objection to near-death experiences.[33] Different people offer different physical descriptions of Jesus, which Greene believes to be problematic. John describes Jesus as having white hair, whereas those who claim to see him in their near-death experiences describe it as brown or black or even blonde.[34] Habermas and Moreland seem to suggest that if John's description of Jesus is to be taken literally, then all descriptions throughout the rest of the book need to be interpreted with the same rigid literalism, such as Jesus being a literal lamb or literal lion.[35]

It should be noted that although Habermas and Moreland do not mention the point, it appears that John did not initially recognize Jesus in the passage despite having interacted with Him after His Resurrection, and no such physical description is given in post-Resurrection Gospel accounts or even in Paul's later encounter with Christ, even though none of the apostles initially recognized him.

Although they feel that Greene committed several philosophical errors in his critique, Habermas and Moreland believed that the worst offense in this regard is his apparent belief that all knowledge must be empirically verified via the scientific method.[36] This seems to be something that was implied rather than outright stated, but Greene appears to suggest that he stood with the medical community at large, which overwhelmingly ignores near-death experiences and seems to be largely disconnected from the popular narratives surrounding them. Greene also points out that near-death experiences are outside the realm of almost all other scientific research, and, therefore, seem to get a pass from those who are near-death experience believers.[37]

The first and most obvious problem they point out with Greene's apparent perspective is that the very statement the only knowable truth is what can be verified scientifically is itself not a statement that can be verified and is, therefore, self-refuting. They

33. Habermas and Moreland, *Beyond Death*, 201.

34 Greene, *If I Should Wake*, 111–12.

35 Habermas and Moreland, *Beyond Death*, 202.

36 Habermas and Moreland, *Beyond Death*, 204.

37. Greene, *If I Should Wake*, 123–24, 295.

believe that even if one was to grant a more lenient interpretation of Greene's implications and assume a softer approach to verification, Greene would be forced to reckon with all the evidence presented thus far, and therefore could not reject near-death experience research for not conforming to a strictly scientific method.[38]

Finally, Green seems to find fault with much of the research into near-death experiences. He unfavorably compares near-death experiences to out-of-body experiences, in general. Although those with either experience (as discussed earlier, these experiences will frequently overlap) may believe that the event has occurred, they are both "personal experiences impossible to corroborate." When researchers attempted to recreate out-of-body experiences, individuals claimed to have or to be able to cause, the researchers overwhelmingly showed that no such event took place, and Greene uses this to cast doubt on both.[39]

Greene expresses his disappointment with researchers of near-death experiences (with Melvin Morse being no exception) for various reasons. These reasons included idealizing accounts of events that may not have occurred, researchers pressuring patients or feeding patients the information desired, and a general lack of objectivity surrounding near-death experience research. To be fair to Greene, he also shows that these tendencies can go too far in the other direction when people are predisposed against the supernatural.[40]

Habermas and Moreland agree with some of Greene's criticisms, but they believe that his view is far too skeptical. They believe that some of the accounts of out-of-body experiences were able to be corroborated and therefore needed to be addressed. Greene, they suggest, must investigate these specific accounts rather than simply ignore them. They seem to imply that Greene's stance prevents him from adding anything beneficial to the discussion of near-death experiences.[41]

---

38 Habermas and Moreland, *Beyond Death*, 204.

39 Greene, *If I Should Wake*, 96–98.

40. Greene, *If I Should Wake*, 70–71.

41 Habermas and Moreland, *Beyond Death*, 205–06.

Objections from an Atheist Perspective

For the atheist perspective, Habermas and Moreland turn to Susan Blackmore because they believed she offered the best analysis beyond focusing on the sensationalized aspects of near-death experiences. Her approach to the research is balanced and she showed in her book a willingness to look at both sides of the argument. Moreland's position seems to be more open to scrutinizing evidential claims for near-death experiences than was Greene's, and they agree with her focus on such reports.[42]

Blackmore is not shy about her naturalism. She makes it clear that the observable universe is all she believes to exist, and her opinions on near-death experiences necessarily fall in line with that belief. Therefore, she believes that what people believe are spiritual experiences are actually mental accommodations made by a dying brain. Because so many of the reported near-death experiences are positive and not all of these reported experiences are actually "near-death," she believes that most are caused by a flood of endorphins from the brain in response to stress.[43]

Habermas and Moreland of course disagree with her reliance on the dying brain or endorphin release to account for near-death experiences. The implication, according to them, is that this would be due to the similar biology of humans. Instead, they believe that this theory at best allows for an either/or situation, where either common biology or the afterlife is a possibility, but the evidence could not strongly rule in favor of one over the other.[44]

As for the argument on people who experience major life changes, particularly positive life changes, Blackmore believes that does not need to point to any sort of spiritual reality. She questions why merely experiencing what an individual believes to be an afterlife should result in people becoming more focused on their spiritual lives Instead, Blackmore again turns to the dying brain hypothesis.

42 Habermas and Moreland, *Beyond Death*, 206.

43. Blackmore, *Dying to Live*, 111–12.

44 Habermas and Moreland, *Beyond Death*, 208.

According to Blackmore, when people dwell on death, whether their own or someone else's, they tend to make positive changes in their lives as a response. When someone is faced with their mortality by almost dying, it should not be surprising when they make those positive changes. Blackmore believes that such confrontation of death, which brings about a realization that there is nothing beyond the current material world, causes fear to be "left behind and life can be lived more fully and directly."[45]

Habermas and Moreland concede that life transformations are by themselves not good evidence that a near-death experience has occurred or that they provide evidence for anything supernatural. Blackmore seems to ignore the reports of increased belief in an afterlife by individuals once they have had a near-death experience rather than having a rejection of it. Instead, people who come to a belief that there is no afterlife are more likely to experience anxiety than peace.

Blackmore's explanation seems to fall flat, not actually providing any substantial reason to reject near-death experiences. She certainly does not offer any reason to downplay the transformations they seem to create in people's lives. According to Habermas and Moreland, she appears to fail to live up to her own standard in her approach to near-death experiences, which demands an explanation of why they feel the way they do.[46]

A Final Defense

Habermas and Moreland make one more defense for the use of near-death experiences in their apologetics, and they use Blackmore's concession of the potential value of a particular event.[47] Blackmore recognizes the power of one claim in particular, that of a woman who, after a near-death experience, was able to describe a tennis shoe sitting on the ledge of the building outside a high window. Her issue with the story is that no independent verification

45 Blackmore, *Dying to Live*, 263.

46. Habermas and Moreland, *Beyond Death*, 209–10.

47 Habermas and Moreland, *Beyond Death*, 212.

of the event exists. Therefore, though the story is fascinating and hits all the marks for what would be needed for a good near-death experience verification, the fact that no one has been able to independently verify the account leaves it as ultimately worthless in the discussion.[48]

The first criticism that Habermas and Moreland level against Blackmore is that she does not make clear what her threshold is for an acceptable level of corroboration. They seem to believe that there is no level of corroboration that would lead her to accept the account. However, Habermas decided to go the extra mile and see what further information he could glean by reaching out to the woman who reported the experience, which he recounted in *Beyond Death*.[49]

Before moving on to Habermas's correspondence, a summary of the initial account is in order. The woman who reported the incident, Kimberly Clark Sharp, was working at a hospital in which a woman, suffered a heart attack and had a near-death experience during which she said to have left her body. Out of concern, Sharp spoke to her and was told about a tennis shoe as evidence that Maria had left her body. Sharp claims she "refused to believe her," but decided to humor her and search for the shoe on the ledge. Famously, she found the shoe just as expected by Maria (and the audience).[50]

Habermas's correspondence with the researcher, Sharp, does add some new information to the more popular narrative surrounding the event. He learned that she was new to the area, and her interview on the subject occurred on the same day that she had her near-death experience. As for the shoe itself, it was hidden, and at no point did she have the opportunity to find it beforehand as it was her first time at that hospital. Not only did she know the location, but she reportedly also was able to describe the shoe in detail.

Habermas believes that most accept to some degree the account relayed by the researcher involved. When other researchers

48 Blackmore, *Dying to Live*, 128.

49. Habermas and Moreland, *Beyond Death*, 213.

50 Sharp, *After the Light*, 9–11.

tried to verify the account, they found the testimony to be consistent. Furthermore, the shoe itself appears to exist (or at least, had existed).[51]

At this point, the discussion returns to some of the previously reported cases, with the main idea appearing to be that what is seen and heard during near-death experiences must find an explanation. With an ever-increasing number of near-death experiences involving being out of the body and cases such as the blind being able to accurately describe what they could suddenly see during their experience. Until such experiences can be explained, they believe that near-death experiences are useful to apologetics and do indeed point to a supernatural reality. They do concede that there are still many questions that can be raised as objections, but the case for naturalism can truly no longer hold up.[52]

51. Habermas and Moreland, *Beyond Death*, 213.
52 Habermas and Moreland, *Beyond Death*, 214–16, 218.

5

Apologetics and Near-Death Experiences

BEFORE EVALUATING THE APOLOGETICS that Habermas has provided, it is worth looking at some of common apologetic methods
and how Habermas employs them in his arguments. His approach
appears to be multifaceted, lending itself to a more effective apologetic. Although there are a wide variety of methods, there are three
that Habermas most commonly employs.

The first approach to mention is an experiential approach to
apologetics. Experientialism is, as the name implies, an appeal to
personal experience to make a truth claim.[1] This is seen in the way
that those who report the near-death experiences are convinced of
the reality of their experience. Regardless of any explanation as to
why the events occurred, they were genuine experiences to those
having them.[2] So strong is the experience that even an ardent atheist who experienced them seem to reject the implications thereof
by sheer force of will.[3] A problem with this method, however, is
that the personal experience of individuals is not a basis for truth,
necessarily.[4]

---

1 Geisler, *Christian Apologetics*, 58.

2. Habermas and Moreland, *Beyond Death*, 207.

3 Ayer, "Postscript to Postmortem."

4 Geisler, *Christian Apologetics*, 70.

The second and most obvious approach Habermas uses is that of evidential apologetics. Evidential apologetics involves using historical events or presents empirical information to make an argument.[5] This occurs every time Habermas and Moreland present information gathered by researchers about those who have had near-death experiences. They rely on the empirical information to present a "minimalistic view of life after death," which they define as providing the information needed to determine that life does indeed continue after one's physical life ends, even though this does not provide any specific details about the afterlife itself.[6] They believed that a minimalistic approach would be fatal to a purely naturalistic worldview.

Ultimately, though these events may be used to attempt to argue for a particular worldview, it is the worldview itself that determines how this information is interpreted.[7] This ties in directly with the final apologetic approach apparent in Habermas's arguments: presuppositionalism. Presuppositionalism is an apologetic method that assumes the Christian worldview is the correct one, and the only correct way to interpret any evidence or to approach logical reasoning is through that lens.[8] The danger becomes when people have these presuppositions and are not aware of them, and then distort information or data based on those presuppositions.[9]

The question is then to what degree does Habermas's own presuppositions affect the way he approaches near-death experiences. He seems to believe that the argument from near-death experiences is a particularly compelling one.[10] So confident is he that he boldly states, "By themselves [near-death experiences] offer evidence that naturalism is mistaken."[11] It should be made clear that he is not arguing for the truth of Christianity (or even theism) based solely on

5 Geisler, *Christian Apologetics*, 72.
6 Habermas and Moreland, *Beyond Death*, 156.
7 Geisler, *Christian Apologetics*, 85.
8. Groothuis, *Christian Apologetics*, 62.
9 Klein, Blomberg, and Hubbard, Jr., *Biblical Interpretation*, 60.
10 Habermas, *Risen Jesus and Future Hope*, 60.
11 Habermas and Licona, *Case for Resurrection of Jesus*, 146.

near-death experiences, but that they are strong enough evidence to reject naturalism. Whether this is true remains to be seen.

THE EVALUATION

Having the case laid out, as well as countering some of the best objections, the time has come to see whether the claims and their evidence hold up to scrutiny and help the apologist make his case against the larger argument for naturalism. There are many naturalists who would like to insist that "extraordinary claims require extraordinary evidence" and this should be the canon for what qualifies as evidence.[12] Should this approach guide the discussion? As discussed above, not necessarily. If the quality of evidence strongly suggests something is true, even if that thing is extraordinary, there is no good reason to reject it merely because the evidence is not as extraordinary as the thing itself.[13]

So, does Habermas's use meet the standard of quality? Is the use of near-death experiences helpful to the Christian apologist? The answers to both seem to be the most frustrating of all: yes and no.

How They Can Be Helpful

Very little time will be given to the "yes" portion of the answers as it veers away from the overall question of using near-death experiences in arguing against naturalism, though the answer itself merits a few words. While it may be tempting to consider apologetics solely a tool of evangelism, it serves an equally important role in both educating and edifying any struggling Christians. Douglas Groothuis wrote in his tome on apologetics, "Apologetics equips questioning or doubting Christians to find the intellectual confidence to be a wise witness to the truth of the gospel."[14]

William Lane Craig went even further in explaining the impact apologetics can have on the life of a believer. He argues that

12 Voss, Helgen, and Jansa, "Extraordinary Claims," 893–98.

13. Craig, *Reasonable Faith*, 270.

14 Groothuis, *Christian Apologetics*, 41.

although the usual Sunday morning mission of helping Christians find intimacy with God to be a good thing, such an emotionally reliant approach does a disservice to the intellect of a Christian, and apologetics helps Christians find nearness to God not only in their hearts but in their minds. An emotional reliance on faith in lieu of intellect also threatens to create shallow Christians, those who do not have true confidence in their faith. This, in turn, causes them to be afraid to evangelize.[15]

When it comes to near-death experiences, they may be helpful to some Christians who are struggling with their faith. Not being able to see the spiritual world can be discouraging, so when people come out of near-death experiences reporting deeply spiritual experiences and changing their lives in a positive and more spiritual way,[16] this could serve to strengthen the faith of Christians. Christians who are strong in their faith are much more likely to evangelize, and that is good for everyone.[17]

How They Are Not Helpful

Despite near-death experiences having some good merits, this section will, unfortunately be the longer of the two. It is well and good if near-death experiences play a role in helping struggling Christians or instilling confidence in their faith, but does that mean they are effective in using them to defend the faith against naturalism or converting the naturalist to at least being open to a supernatural realm? In the case of near-death experiences, the answer seems to be a safe, though tentative, "no."

Unfortunately, Habermas's focus on near-death experiences seems entirely on how they can be used apologetically in an evangelism context, and that is where they appear to begin to fail. Foremost seems to be the issue of the popular accounts of near-death experiences. When individuals report lights, feelings of bliss,

15   Craig, *Reasonable Faith*, 19–21.

16.   Habermas and Moreland, *Beyond Death*, 208.

17   Craig, *Reasonable Faith*, 21.

encountering angelic beings or deceased relatives, etcetera;[18] these accounts still inform the larger narrative of what it means to have a near-death experience, and these cannot be ignored. Habermas may attempt to claim that such accounts are of little concern to him because he would rather focus on what is verifiable or has appropriate substantiation,[19] but this position is not entirely tenable.

Even in Habermas's examples, many of these events occur. In the example of Katie, she claimed a visit to Heaven and an encounter not only with Jesus but with God the Father as well. In the case of Rick, he not only describes a feeling of intense bliss and following a light (which he abandons in fear of permanent death), but he also describes a strange sort of possession of his sister's body, watching events unfold from her eyes.[20] Although there are many examples of near-death experiences and some of them do not necessarily include some of the same details as the popular accounts, they are part of so many that seems clear that they are indeed an integral part of the experiences as a whole. It is also possible, as seen in the example of Rick, that some of these details were simply not reported in the repeated account.[21]

The apparent reasons that Habermas decides to forgo a discussion on these events are most likely twofold. The first is that they would be nearly impossible to verify. The mere fact that the majority of cases report these elements does not mean they point to any sort of spiritual reality, which is why Habermas must turn to things that have some element in the real world, such as leaving the body to observe things in the same or a different room.[22]

The second is that research is closing in on answers to these phenomena and that is, quite frankly, harmful to the case for near-death experiences as being something spiritual. In one study, high levels of carbon dioxide appeared to account for some of the experiences because the carbon dioxide acted as a hallucinogen. They also

---

18   Long, "Near-Death Experience," 372.

19.   Habermas, *Risen Jesus and Future Hope*, 60.

20   Morse and Perry, *Closer to the Light*, 3–6, 177–178.

21   Habermas and Moreland, *Beyond Death*, 158.

22   Habermas, *The Risen Jesus and Future Hope*, 60.

found that those who already had a near-death experience were much more likely to report another one.[23] Another study seemed to indicate that those who suffer from severe migraines may be more prone to near-death experiences or similar events, again indicating a biological cause for much of what is reported.[24] There are even studies that suggest certain psychological attributes may play a role, with one such study suggesting those who are more prone to having false memories are also more prone to having a near-death experience.[25] With these and other studies, both discussed above and many that have not been, it appears that much of the puzzle is beginning to come into focus and it is now simply a matter of correctly putting the pieces together.

Moving on to what Habermas considers more viable evidence, which has been discussed at length above, problems persist. Although there are various sources on both sides of the debate, it is worth focusing on Habermas's sources of Greene and Blackmore. The way he (and by extension, Moreland) approaches the two shows the very beginnings of the problems as they appear to be.

First, the opinion expressed of Greene's approach is fairly dismissive. When discussing whether the atheist (Blackmore) or the Christian (Greene) has the better approach to near-death experiences, they wrote, "We will pay more attention to [Blackmore], who treats it far more thoughtfully, while Greene prefers to dismiss rather offhandedly even the possibility of such data. We find Greene's attitude rather cavalier, since he is a scientist who repeatedly calls for empirical, measurable results."[26] Even though this could be characterized as dismissing dismissiveness, the possible reasoning behind Greene's position should be considered more carefully.

There is a well-known fallacy known as the "straw man" fallacy. This fallacy entails setting up or distorting an opponent's argument in order to easily refute it. Such a fallacy is usually done by taking the premise of an argument and making it sound almost the same,

23. Klemenc-Ketis, Kersnik, and Grmec, "Effect of Carbon Dioxide," 4–6.

24 Kondziella et al., "Migraine Aura," 11–12.

25 Martial et al., "False Memory Susceptibility," 814.

26. Habermas and Moreland, *Beyond Death*, 210.

but in a way that can be easily rejected.[27] Douglas Groothuis offers an example of a straw man fallacy in explaining the cosmological argument for the existence of God.

The first premise of a common form of the argument is "Whatever begins to exist has a cause," which is often restated as "Everything that exists must have a cause." Although these two may sound similar, they are at their essence completely different questions, and the latter would appear to refute the theist's own position.[28]

The purpose of bringing up the straw man fallacy is not to suggest that Habermas or Moreland engage in this fallacy. Instead, it shows its opposite: setting up an opponent's argument in the strongest way possible in order to show the strength of one's own argument. This is exemplified in an interview Ben Shapiro had with William Lane Craig in which Craig lays out his versions of the Kalam cosmological argument and the moral argument. After letting him make his case, Shapiro asked him to "steelman" an opponent's counterarguments in the best way possible.[29]

Giving Greene the benefit of the doubt, this would be a reasonable thing for him to strive for and could very well account for his rigid attitude on the subject. In the conclusion of his book, he offers some reasons for his rejection of near-death experiences, which in itself shows why he would want to steelman his opponent's argument. His fear is that near-death experiences can actually have an opposite affect and lead people to New Age or occult beliefs. He wrote, "For the non-Christian, the NDE [near-death experience] can lead to the ultimate rejection of Jesus and eternal separation from God."[30]

Susan Blackmore may have been doing the same thing as she developed her hypothesis that near-death experiences are caused by a dying brain. In order to fortify her own position, she needed to address what she conceived as being her hypothesis's foremost challenge: claims of out-of-body experiences in the midst of a

27 Hansen, "Fallacies."

28. Groothuis, *Christian Apologetics*, 209, 214.

29 Shapiro, "William Lane Craig."

30. Greene, *If I Should Wake*, 298.

near-death experience. If this is a valid experience, then any naturalistic explanation would fail in light of this.[31] Although Habermas clearly appreciates the more open approach that Blackmore takes in this regard,[32] it may be safer to simply regard her approach as creating a "steelman fallacy" against which her argument must hold up rather than a larger allowance for the argument in favor of near-death experiences.

It is important to realize that even as a naturalist Blackmore does not ignore the fact that near-death experiences are, at least to the individual having them, valid experiences. It does not mean, according to her, that there was any sort of spiritual event or even any spiritual significance to be attached to that event. She believes the reason people with these experiences wish to attach a greater significance to them beyond the natural is to add legitimacy to the reality of their experiences.[33]

Habermas relies almost entirely on the out-of-body aspects of near-death experiences. All these experiences were reported in interviews with those who had the experience and required some sort of corroboration of what they claimed to have seen and heard while out of their bodies.[34] Anyone who is exploring this topic must then ask if such accounts are enough to believe that near-death experiences are sufficient to be used as evidence of the supernatural.

It is the fact that people are being interviewed about their memories of the experience that concerns Greene. He is concerned that this sort of process prevents rigorous scientific study. This is not, however, the full extent of his concern. His greater concern seems to be that the interview process is more "art" than "science," and by its very nature subjective.[35] Habermas asks why near-death experiences should be subjected to scientific investigation as there is no way to schedule and plan such an investigation,[36] but it seems

31 Blackmore, *Dying to Live*, 111.

32 Habermas and Moreland, *Beyond Death*, 210.

33. Blackmore, *Dying to Live*, 128.

34 Habermas, *Risen Jesus and Future Hope*, 60–61.

35 Greene, *If I Should Wake*, 295–96.

36 Habermas and Moreland, *Beyond Death*, 204.

that there should be more inquiry about the veracity of the interview process.

Blackmore offers further challenges to the narratives behind those who leave their bodies during a near-death experience. First, she points out that memory can often be faulty, and people tend to remember the retelling of an event rather than the event itself; with each retelling, the more real that event will seem to the individual—whether it actually was real or not. Evidential testimony that seems concrete is then suddenly in doubt.

Second, those who have been resuscitated after a near-death experience may have had prior knowledge of what medical procedures were performed. They may also have been resuscitated and seen the people around them and the equipment around that which was just in use and be able to piece together with accuracy what happened. When researchers attempt to look back at the medical records to verify, it is standard procedure to be as concise as possible rather than fill out a detailed report of every detail, so there would be no way to know whether the details of these accounts are accurate.

Finally, possibly the most relevant point she brings up is that there is currently no way of knowing how much information the individual is receiving through his body. Even a little bit of information can lead to people creating an entire narrative with what seem to be very concrete details. In this same way, those who are having a near-death experience may have their bodies pick up sounds and feelings around them and can create very concrete and possibly accurate retellings of what occurred, including the medical procedures.[37]

All claims made by Habermas rely entirely on eyewitness accounts. In the world of legal scholars, eyewitnesses pose a major problem for prosecutors and defenders alike. Memory failure of events and details is common, and the memories can often become distorted over time. Although in this world judges seem to be reluctant to acknowledge this, the experts in the field fear that eyewitness testimony is inaccurate enough that people are often wrongly

37. Blackmore, *Dying to Live*, 116, 117–18, 122–24.

convicted and there need to be reforms in their acceptance.[38] If eyewitness accounts are so commonly wrong, how can a case be built if there is a dependence on self-reported accounts verified by eyewitnesses?

In the case of Katie, her doctor was the one who verified her account by virtue of simply being there and recalling that what Katie reported was true. Her family had to recall the events of the stressful night before to affirm that her distant out of body experiences were true.[39] In the case of Maria and her shoe, the one case Habermas seems to think is the heavyweight claim to overcome all opposition, relies only on the report of the researcher herself, Kimberly Clark Sharp. Even in Habermas's own follow-up on the story he only speaks to Sharp, Maria herself is never spoken to in any context.[40]

Even the researchers themselves can be called into question over their motives. Morse was attempting to justify his grant money to research near-death experiences.[41] Sharp had a deep personal interest in near-death experiences as she had one herself only a few years prior.

Although the details of her own experience are not necessary to recount here, the fact that she had one would certainly give her some motivation to affirm other near-death experiences, despite her protestations to the contrary.[42] A few years after she had reported the event, she would start a major near-death experience research organization and would publish two books and write several articles on the subject.[43]

In no way should any of this be taken as a suggestion that anyone is lying. Even granting that all events are true, there are clearly enough problems for the atheist to point out. At best, the atheist can point to the advancement of medical research and the

---

38. Jenkins, *Analysis of Elizabeth F. Loftus,* 23–25.

39. Morse and Perry, *Closer to the Light,* 3–6.

40 Habermas and Moreland, *Beyond Death,* 212–14.

41 Morse and Perry, *Closer to the Light,* 48–50.

42. Sharp, *The Spiritual Path,* viii—ix, 10.

43 Sharp, *What I Discovered;* Sharp, *The Spiritual Path.*

explanations for why those with near-death experiences can have such amazing reports and reject near-death experiences as simply being too unknown to be properly understood, forcing the theist to take a God-of-the-gaps approach to the subject. At worst, the atheist could use near-death experiences to point to the success of those who do work in near-death experiences as being fraudulent and make a mockery of theists and do damage to the good work of apologists in the other argument they have made.

This is not a merely hypothetical scenario. Sharp herself was one of several targets of an atheist hoax when an atheist, Thomas Westbrook, faked a near-death experience. His account was published on a near-death experience research site and made a mockery of everyone who has ever had such an experience. What was the conclusion from an atheist promoting the work? Those who do work with near-death experiences do so in hopes of being able to "sell it and make millions."[44] Appearing to have reasonable explanations for all, or at least most, of the various aspects of near-death experiences, then despite the value that they may have in the life of the Christian, it does not appear to have any true value in evangelism and apologetics. Furthermore, this seems to pose a larger problem to Christianity as a whole, particularly as it casts such doubts on eyewitnesses.

It is, after all, the account of eyewitnesses is the foundation of belief in the Resurrection of Jesus Christ. If eyewitnesses are to be doubted, can the Resurrection be believed? If the Resurrection cannot be believed, then (as it is written in 1 Corinthians 15:14), is it true that "our preaching is in vain, and your faith is in vain"?

A Comparison to the Claims of Jesus' Resurrection

Much was made of the use of eyewitness in the above discussion of the nature of evidence and claims. Pointing to both the miracle at Fatima[45] as well as the Resurrection, eyewitnesses were used to argue

44. Hall, "Near-Death Experiences Explained."

45. The miracle at Fatima will not receive further consideration in this book as it is not central to the Christian faith, which is ultimately what is at

against a Humean approach to evidence. Is this then a contradictory position to hold, and does it follow that accepting the eyewitness accounts of the Resurrection necessitates an acceptance of the same from near-death experiences or vice versa? Surely, it is not.

It was also asked above how much corroboration would be enough for a Humian naturalist to accept a miracle, and Habermas asks the same question of Blackmore in her skepticism over Sharp's account of Maria.[46] As pointed out above, it is an easier thing to reject the narratives of near-death experiences considering that there is personal or financial incentive to make these reports. Furthermore, it would be reasonable for someone to ask, "What is the cost of reporting near-death experiences?" The answer appears to be that there is none.

This is a completely different scenario than that faced by the eyewitnesses of the Resurrection. To help make the case for just how different it is and why that early testimony can be believed, one needs to simply turn back to Habermas. His extensive work on the Resurrection, as well as others, will provide an excellent counterbalance to his own work on near-death experiences. Although there is much to say about the Resurrection, a full treatment thereof is outside the scope of this book, so only the most relevant of these points will be discussed.

First, the disciples truly believed that their friend, Jesus, appeared to them. Although one could quickly object that those with near-death experiences truly believe their experiences were real, the cost of such belief is quite different from that of the disciples. The disciples, in their constant proclamation of their belief, faced ongoing "imprisonment, torture, and martyrdom."[47]

This belief that the disciples had also instilled a massive change within the disciples. Again, even if one were to claim that the same is true of those who had near-death experiences, the fact is the disciples went from being afraid of government authorities

---

stake in this discussion.

46 Habermas and Moreland, *Beyond Death*, 213.

47. Habermas and Licona, *Case for Resurrection of Jesus*, 49–50.

to boldly spreading the message of a risen Christ in the face of all opposition.[48]

Second, there was a physical empty tomb to which the disciples could point, unlike accounts of near-death experiences that can pass off general accounts as being authentic. Because Jesus was crucified and then buried in specific locations in Jerusalem, when the disciples began to preach a risen Jesus the Roman and Jewish authorities alike could have easily pointed to the body of Jesus had the tomb not been empty. The disciples were accused of stealing the body, a highly unlikely event, and this accusation was a de facto admission of the tomb being empty. There is also the fact that the earliest reports of the Resurrection came from women. In the time and place this occurred, women's testimony was considered quite weak, and claiming that women were the first to see the risen Christ would not have helped the cause, and really the only motivation for including it would be that it was true.[49]

William Lane Craig helps take this point further. Whereas those who report near-death experiences are reporting a personal experience that only they had and is corroborated by those involved (such as the doctor or the direct family member), the accounts of the empty tomb were by multiple independent sources. This includes the written and separate accounts by the Gospel writers, by the accounts in Acts, by Paul, and many of these written accounts clearly use language that comes from even older creeds from the church. There is also the matter of the claims that Jesus appeared to five hundred people as well as "all of the apostles," all of whom could give the same account of the risen Jesus.[50]

There should be no need to doubt the account of the eyewitness of the Resurrection. Though the accounts of those with near-death experiences could reasonably be challenged by naturalists, the standards that they would apply to them would not be relevant here. There is absolutely no way anyone could claim that money is a financial motivation when the governments of the time were

---

48 Groothuis, *Christian Apologetics*, 551–52.

49 Habermas and Licona, *Case for Resurrection of Jesus*, 70–71, 73.

50. Craig, *Reasonable Faith*, 365–66, 378, 380.

so actively persecuting the Christian faith. The tables are not so easily turned.

SUMMARY

If the objective of using near-death experience accounts in apologetics is to strengthen the faith of the Christian, then they certainly have their place. Strengthening the faith of Christians in order to make them bold proclaimers of the Gospel is an admirable and necessary thing, and it is one of the reasons why apologetics is so important as a whole.[51] Unfortunately, it seems that their value ends there.

When it comes to evangelizing through apologetics, near-death experiences would seem to do far more harm than good. Greene's concern that a fascination with near-death experiences can lead to the occult (or spiritualism) rather than to Christ is a valid concern, and their vague nature certainly allows for that possibility.[52] Blackmore's explanations as to why particular events reported during the experience could be reported with accuracy further points to nature catching up with concrete answers, and these explanations would need to face a much tougher challenge.[53] Also considering the nature of individual eyewitness accounts and their problems,[54] it would be prudent to avoid using near-death experiences as evidence against naturalism, especially in light of other arguments Christians have at their disposal.

51 Craig, *Reasonable Faith*, 19–21.

52. Greene, *If I Should Wake*, 298.

53 Blackmore, *Dying to Live*, 116, 117–18, 122–24.

54 Jenkins, *Analysis of Elizabeth F. Loftus*, 23–25.

The Final Word

FOR EVERY HUMAN ON earth, the clock is ticking towards their inevitable death. Whether one lives to the oldest of ages (expiring quietly) or if death comes suddenly (in any of the myriad of ways people die), the end of biological life is the ultimate outcome for everyone. For the Christian, however, there is the expectation of continuation beyond this fleeting life on earth. Naturalists have no such optimism and can only hope that their time on earth is a pleasant one. Because Christians have a divine assurance, they want to share that hope with others. Still, theological questions remain: Can near-death experiences help lead those far from Christ to Him? Can they be added to the repertoire of Apologetic arguments for Christianity?

There is certainly a degree of fascination with the power of near-death experiences, as atheists like A. J. Ayer can attest. His own experience caused him to question the finality of life after departing this mortal coil.[1] It must be remembered that even in this powerful personal experience, Ayer remained an atheist.[2] If even a personal experience could not dissuade this skeptic, then can any amount of reasoning from near-death experiences succeed? This common response should not surprise any Christian as the Bible itself says in Luke 16:31, "If they do not listen to Moses and the prophets, neither will they be convinced even if someone rises from the dead."

---

1. Ayer, "What I Saw," 39.
2 Ayer, "Postscript to Postmortem," 206.

SEEING THE LIGHT

There have been many reasons given for rejecting near-death experiences in Apologetics. This should not be cause for concern, for the Christian faith is filled with a rich history of excellent thinking concerning near-death experiences that relies on something far greater than mere reported personal experiences of others. Habermas himself agrees that they are only a part of a larger cumulative case against naturalism.[3]

Other stronger arguments for the Christian faith are at the apologist's disposal. Anselm wrote an argument that was based entirely on human reason for the existence of God so that even the atheist would have to conclude that, logically, God must exist.[4] William Lane Craig has in much more recent years brought the Kalam cosmological argument to the forefront, using not only reason but also modern science to bring people to the conclusion that God must exist.[5] There are also, as shown above, excellent reasons for believing in the Resurrection of Jesus, the lynchpin of the Christian faith.

This by no means covers all the different arguments for God and for Christianity; it merely provides examples of the many arguments that actually exist. Therefore, if the use of near-death experiences is mostly ineffective and there are so many other arguments that exist, then why include them as part of the argument at all? It seems that their use would risk undermining the larger case that is being made.

Jesus Christ is the true God, and He historically rose from the grave, and that is where all Apologetic endeavors must ultimately lead. Through Jesus' sacrifice on the Cross and His Resurrection, God conquered death, saved humanity from the dark domain of mortality, and restored the broken relationship between Him and His children.

3 Habermas, *Risen Jesus and Future Hope*, 62.
4 Dulles, *History of Apologetics*, 101.
5 Craig, *Reasonable Faith*, 111–12.

82

Bibliography

Agence French-Presse. "'Dead' Man Comes Alive Moments Before Autopsy." *IOL* (2021).

Aleman, André, and Edward H.F. de Haan. "Fantasy Proneness, Mental Imagery and Reality Monitoring." *Personality and Individual Differences* 36.8 (2004) 1747–54. https://doi.org/10.1016/j.paid.2003.07.011.

Ayer, A. J. "Postscript to Postmortem." *Spectator* (1988) 205–08. http://archive. spectator.co.uk/article/15th-october-1988/13/postscript-to-a-postmortem.

———. "What I Saw When I Was Dead." *National Review* 40.20 (1988) 38–40.

Barber, Paul. "The Real Vampire." In *Bram Stroker's Dracula: A Documentary Journey into Vampire Country and the* Dracula *Phenomenon.* Edited by Elizabeth Miller, 52–56. New York: Pegasus Books, 2009.

Blackmore, Susan. *Dying to Live: Near-Death Experiences.* Buffalo: Prometheus Books, 1993.

Britton, Willoughby B., and Richard R. Bootzin. "Near-Death Experiences and the Temporal Lobe." *Psychological Science* 15.4 (2004) 254–58. https://doi. org/10.1111/j.0956-7976.2004.00661.x.

Bush, Nancy Evans and Bruce Greyson. "Distressing Near-Death Experiences: The Basics." *Missouri Medicine* 111.6 (2014) 486–91.

Cassol, Helena, Benoît Pétré, Sophie Degrange, Charlotte Martial, Vanessa Charland-Verville, François Lallier, Isabelle Bragard, Michèle Guillaume, and Steven Laureys. "Qualitative Thematic Analysis of the Phenomenology of Near-Death Experiences." *PLoS ONE* 13.2 (2018) e0193001. https://doi. org/10.1371/journal.pone.0193001.

Cassol, Helena, Charlotte Martial, Jitka Annen, Géraldine Martens, Vanessa Charland-Verville, Steve Majerus, and Steven Laureys. "A Systematic Analysis of Distressing Near-death Experience Accounts." *Memory* 28.8 (2019) 1122–29. https://dx.doi.org/10.1080/09658211.2019.1626438.

Challies, Tim. "Heaven Tourism." *Challies* (2012). https://www.challies.com/ articles/heaven-tourism/.

Chandradasa, Miyuru, Chamara Wijesinghe, A. L. A. Kuruppuarachchi, and Mahendra Perera. "Near-Death Experiences in a Multi-Religious Hospital Population in Sri Lanka." *Journal of Religion and Health* 57.5 (2018) 1599–605.

Charlier, Philippe. "Oldest Medical Description of a near Death Experience (NDE), France, 18th Century." *Resuscitation* 85.9 (2014) e155. https://www-sciencedirect-com.ezproxy.liberty.edu/science/article/pii/S0300957214005887.

Chopra, Deepak. *Life After Death: The Burden of Proof.* New York: Random House, 2006.

Cook, Kymberli, Mikel Del Rosario, Gary Habermas, and Daniel Hill. "What Happens When We Die?" In *The Table Podcast* 26.05 (2020). https://voice.dts.edu/tablepodcast/what-happens-when-we-die/.

Craig, William Lane. *On Guard: Defending Your Faith with Reason and Precision.* Colorado Springs: David C. Cook, 2010.

———. *Reasonable Faith: Christian Truth and Apologetics.* Wheaton: Crossway, 2008.

Daniel, Clement and Anne Donnet. "Migrainous Complex Hallucinations in a 17-Year-Old Adolescent." *Headache: The Journal of Head and Face Pain* 51 (2011) 999–1001. https://doi.org/10.1111/j.1526-4610.2010.01823.x.

Dedrick, Carrie. "Why are Christians so Fascinated with Heaven Tourism?" *Crosswalk* (2011). https://www.crosswalk.com/blogs/christian-trends/why-are-christians-so-fascinated-with-heaven-tourism.html.

Deming, David. "Do Extraordinary Claims Require Extraordinary Evidence?" *Philosophia* 44.4 (2016) 1319–31.

Dimond, Bridgit. "The Clinical Definition of Death and the Legal Implications for Staff." *British Journal of Nursing* 13.7 (2004) 391–93.

Dossey, Larry. "The Undead: Botched Burials, Safety Coffins, and the Fear of the Grave." *Explore* 3.4 (2007) 347–54. https://doi.org/10.1016/j.explore.2007.05.001.

Dulles, Avery. *A History of Apologetics.* San Francisco: Ignatius, 2005.

Fischer, John Martin, and Benjamin Mitchell-Yellin. *Near-Death Experiences: Understanding Visions of the Afterlife.* Oxford: Oxford University Press, 2016.

Flew, Anthony. "Neo-Humean Arguments about the Miraculous." In *In Defense of Miracles: A Comprehensive Case for God's Action in History.* Edited by R. Douglas Geivett and Gary R. Habermas, 45–57. Downers Grove: InterVarsity, 1997.

Geisler, Norman L. *Christian Apologetics.* Grand Rapids: Baker Academic, 2013.

———. "Miracle and the Modern Mind." In *In Defense of Miracles: A Comprehensive Case for God's Action in History,* edited by R. Douglas Geivett and Gary R. Habermas, 73–75. Downers Grove: InterVarsity, 1997.

Graham, Ruth. "'I Did Not Die. I Did Not Go to Heaven:' How the controversy around a Christian bestseller engulfed the evangelical publishing industry—and tore a family apart." *Slate* (2014). https://slate.com/human-interest/2019/07/the-boy-who-came-back-from-heaven-christian-book-scandal.html.

Greene, H. Leone. *If I Should Wake Before I Die: The Biblical and Medical Truth About Near-Death Experiences.* Wheaton: Crossway Books, 1997.

Groothuis, Douglas. *Christian Apologetics: A Comprehensive Case of Biblical Faith.* Downers Grove: InterVarsity, 2011.

Habermas, Gary R. *The Risen Jesus and Future Hope*. Lanham: Rowman & Littlefield, 2003.

Habermas, Gary and J. P. Moreland. *Beyond Death: Exploring the Evidence for Immortality*. Eugene: Wipf and Stock, 2004.

Habermas, Gary R. and Michael R. Licona. *The Case for the Resurrection of Jesus*. Grand Rapids: Kregel, 2004.

Hall, Andrew. "Near-Death Experiences Explained." *Patheos* (2017). https://www.patheos.com/blogs/laughingindisbelief/2017/06/near-death-experiences-explained/.

Hansen, Hans. "Fallacies." The Stanford Encyclopedia of Philosophy (2020). https://plato.stanford.edu/archives/sum2020/entries/fallacies/.

Hawkes, David. "Extraordinary Claims Don't Always Require Extraordinary Evidence, but They Do Require Good Quality Evidence." *Asian Pacific Journal of Cancer Prevention* 20.7 (2019) 1935–37. https://dx.doi.org/doi:10.31557/APJCP.2019.20.7.1935.

Heaps, Christopher, and Michael Nash. "Individual Differences in Imagination Inflation." *Psychonomic Bulletin & Review* 6.2 (1999) 313–18. https://dx.doi.org/10.3758/BF03214120.

Hume, David. "Of Miracles." In *In Defense of Miracles: A Comprehensive Case for God's Action in History*. Edited by R. Douglas Geivett and Gary R. Habermas, 27–44. Downers Grove: InterVarsity, 1997.

Jenkins, William J. *An Analysis of Elizabeth F. Loftus's: Eyewitness Testimony*. London: Macat International, 2017. https://doi-org.ezproxy.liberty.edu/10.4324/9781912282500.

Johnson, Christine D. "'Heaven Is for Real' hits major sales milestone." *Christian Retailing*. (2014). https://www.christianretailing.com/index.php/newsletter/latest/27680-heaven-is-for-real-hits-major-sales-milestone.

Jong, Jonathan, Jamin Halberstadt, and Matthias Bluemke. "Foxhole Atheism, Revisited: The Effects of Mortality Salience on Explicit and Implicit Religious Belief." *Journal of Experimental Social Psychology* 48.5 (2012) 983–89.

Kaiser, Eric A., Aleksandra Igdalova, Geoffrey K Aguirre, and Brett Cucchiara, "A Web-Based, Branching Logic Questionnaire for the Automated Classification of Migraine." *Cephalalgia* 39.10 (2019) 1257–66. https://doi.org/10.1177/0333102419847749.

Khoshab, Hadi, Seyedhamid Seyedbagheri, Sedigheh Iranmanesh, Parvin Mangolian Shahrbabaki, Mahlagha Dehghan, Batool Tirgari, and Seyed Habibollah Hosseini. "Near-Death Experience among Iranian Muslim Cardiopulmonary Resuscitation Survivors." *Iranian Journal of Nursing & Midwifery Research* 25.5 (2020) 414–18. https://doi.org/10.4103/ijnmr.IJNMR_190_19.

"Kimberly Clark Sharp, MSW, LCSW." *Seattle International Association for Near-Death Studies*. https://seattleiands.org/kimberly-clark-sharp.html.

Klein, William W., Craig L. Blomberg, and Robert L. Hubbard, Jr. *Introduction to Biblical Interpretation*. Grand Rapids: Zondervan, 2017.

Klemenc-Ketis, Zalika, Janko Kersnik, and Stefek Grmec. "The Effect of Carbon Dioxide on Near-Death Experiences in out-of-Hospital Cardiac Arrest Survivors: A Prospective Observational Study." *Critical Care* (London, England) 14.2 (2010) 1–7. https://www.ncbi.nlm.nih.gov/pubmed/20377847.

Kondziella, Daniel, Jens P. Dreier, and Markus Harboe Olsen. "Prevalence of Near-Death Experiences in People with and without REM Sleep Intrusion." *Peer Journal* 7.e7585 (2019) 1–17. Accessed May 12, 2021. https://doi.org/10.7717/peerj.7585.

Kondziella, Daniel, Markus Harboe Olsen, Coline L. Lemale, and Jens P. Dreier. "Migraine Aura, a Predictor of near-Death Experiences in a Crowdsourced Study." *Peer Journal* 7.e8202 (2019) 1–23. https://doi.org/10.7717/peerj.8202.

Koch, Christof. "Tales of the Dying Brain." *Scientific American* 322.6 (2020) 33–37.

Levitan, Harold. "Dreams Which Culminate in Migraine Headaches." Psychotherapy and Psychosomatics 41.4 (1984) 161–66.

Lizza, John P. "Defining Death: Beyond Biology." *Diametros* 55.3 (2018) 1–19.

Long, Jeffrey. "Near-Death Experience: Evidence for Their Reality." *Missouri Medicine: Journal of the Missouri State Medical Association* 111.5 (2014) 372–80.

Long, Jeffrey and Janice Miner Holden. "Does the Arousal System Contribute to Near-Death and Out-of-Body Experiences? A Summary and Response." *Journal of Near-Death Studies* 25.3 (2007) 135–69. https://dx.doi.org/10.1212/01.wnl.0000252725.89247.7b.

Martial, Charlotte, Vanessa Charland-Verville, Hedwidge Dehon, and Steven Laureys. "False Memory Susceptibility in Coma Survivors With and Without a Near-Death Experience." *Psychological Research* 82 (2017) 806–18. https://doi-org.ezproxy.liberty.edu/10.1007/s00426–017-0855–9.

Martial, Charlotte, Héléna Cassol, Vanessa Charland-Verville, Harald Merckelbach, and Steven Laureys. "Fantasy Proneness Correlates with the Intensity of Near-Death Experience." *Frontiers in Psychiatry* 9.190 (2018) 1–7.

Martial, Charlotte, Hélena Cassol, Georgios Antonopoulos, Thomas Charlier, Julien Heros, Anne-Françoise Donneau, Vanessa Charland-Verville, and Steven Laureys. "Temporality of Features in Near-Death Experience Narratives." *Frontiers in Human Neuroscience* 11.211 (2017) 1–9. https://dx.doi.org/10.3389/fnhum.2017.00311.

Malarkey, Alex, and The News Division. "'The Boy Who Came Back From Heaven' Recants Story, Rebukes Christian Retailers." *Pulpit and Pen* (2015). https://pulpitandpen.org/2015/01/13/the-boy-who-came-back-from-heaven-recants-story-rebukes-christian-retailers/.

Martin, Sean. "Near Death Experience: Woman sees God in Space in Afterlife Claims." *Express* (2020). https://www.express.co.uk/news/weird/1326931/near-death-experience-afterlife-proof-of-god-space-nde.

McNabb, Tyler Dalton and Joseph E. Blado. "Mary and Fátima: A Modest C-Inductive Argument for Catholicism." *Perichoresis: The Theological Journal of Emanuel University* 18.5 (2020) 55–65. https://dx.doi.org/10.2478/perc-2020-0028.

Merckelbach, Harold, Robert Horselenberg, and Peter Muris. "The Creative Experiences Questionnaire (CEQ): a Brief Self-Report Measure of Fantasy Proneness." *Personality and Individual Differences* 31.6 (2001) 987–95. https://doi.org/10.1016/S0191-8869(00)00201-4.

Miles, Steven. "Death in a Technological and Pluralistic Culture." In *The Definition of Death: Contemporary Controversies.* Edited by Stuart J. Youngner, Robert M. Arnold, and Renie Schapiro, 312–18. Baltimore: Johns Hopkins University Press, 1999.

"Miracles from Heaven (2016)." *Box Office Mojo.* https://www.boxofficemojo.com/title/tt4257926/

Moody, Raymond A. "Getting Comfortable with Death & Near-Death Experiences: Near-Death Experiences: An Essay in Medicine & Philosophy." *Missouri Medicine* 110.5 (2013) 368–71.

Morse, Melvin, and Paul Perry. *Closer to the Light: Learning from the Near-Death Experiences of Children.* New York: Ballantine Books, 1990.

Mortenson, Terry. "The Religion of Naturalism." in *World Religions and Cults: Atheistic and Humanistic Religions.* Edited by Bodie Hodge and Roger Patterson (205–26). Green Forest: Master Books, 2016. Kindle.

Nelson, Kevin R., Michelle Mattingly, Sherman A. Lee, and Frederick A. Schmitt. "Does The Arousal System Contribute to Near Death Experience?" *Neurology* 66.7 (2006) 1003–09. https://dx.doi.org/10.1212/01.wnl.0000204296.15607.37.

Presinger, Michael A. "Religious and Mystical Experiences as Artifacts of Temporal Lobe Function: A General Hypothesis." *Perceptual and Motor Skills* 53.3 (1983) 1255–62. https://dx.doi.org/10.2466/pms.1983.57.3f.1255.

Purtill, Richard L. "Defining Miracles." In *In Defense of Miracles: A Comprehensive Case for God's Action in History.* Edited by R. Douglas Geivett and Gary R. Habermas (61–72). Downers Grove: InterVarsity, 1997.

Rawlings, Maurice. *Beyond Death's Door.* Nashville: Thomas Nelson, 1978.

Reville, William. "Near Death Experience: The Phenomenon of the Mind 'Leaving' the Body." *The Irish Times* (2020). https://www.irishtimes.com/news/science/near-death-experience-the-phenomenon-of-the-mind-leaving-the-body-1.4345638.

Ring, Kenneth. "Solving the Riddle of Frightening Near-Death Experiences: Some Testable Hypotheses and a Perspective Based on *A Course in Miracles.*" *Journal of Near-Death Studies* 13.2 (1995) 5–23. https://dx.doi.org/doi:10.17514/JNDS-1994-13-1-p5-23.

Roediger, Henry L. and Kathleen B. McDermott. "Creating False Memories: Remembering Words Not Presented in Lists." *Journal of Experimental Psychology* 21.4 (1995) 803–14. https://dx.doi.org/10.1037/0278-7393.21.4.803.

Sagan, Carl. "Encyclopaedia Galactica." *Cosmos: A Personal Voyage* 12 (1980) 1:12. https://www.youtube.com/watch?v=llZNU799lOg.

———. "The Shores of the Cosmic Ocean." *Cosmos: A Personal Voyage*. Episode 1 (1980) 3:12. https://www.youtube.com/watch?v=p3hRWM1y5CQ&list =PL6rj1b7vga5WdZBLyql4pprGRUmXUceBn.

Saunders, David Michael, Brian Fallon Norko, James Phillips, Jenifer Nields, Salman Majeed, Joseph Merlino, and Fayez El-Gabalawi. "Varieties of Religious (Non)Affiliation: A Primer for Mental Health Practitioners on the 'Spiritual but Not Religious' and the 'Nones." *The Journal of Nervous and Mental Disease* 208.5 (2020) 424–430. https://dx.doi.org/10.1097/ NMD.0000000000001141.

Shapiro, Ben. "William Lane Craig | The Ben Shapiro Show Sunday Special Ep. 50." *The Daily Wire* (2019) 13:32. https://www.youtube.com/watch?v=hL-zJzE5clA&t=812s.

Sharp, Kimberly Clark. *After the Light: The Spiritual Path to Purpose*. New York: Avon Books, 1995.

Sharp, Kimberly Clark. *After the Light: What I Discovered on the Other Side of Life That Can Change Your World*. iUniverse, 2003. Kindle.

Shushan, Gregory. *Conceptions of the Afterlife in Early Civilizations: Universalism, Constructivism and near-Death Experience*. London: Bloomsbury, 2011.

Tressoldi, Patrizio E. "Extraordinary Claims Require Extraordinary Evidence: The Case of Non-Local Perception, a Classical and Bayesian Review of Evidences." *Frontiers in Psychology* 2 (2011) 1–5. https://dx.doi.org/10.3389 /fpsyg.2011.00117.

van Lommel, Pirn, Ruud van Wees, Vincent Meyers, and Ingrid Elfferich. "Near-Death Experience in Survivors of Cardiac Arrest: A Prospective Study in the Netherlands." *The Lancet* 358.9298 (2001) 2039–45.

Vardamis, A. A., and J. E. Owens. "Ernest Hemingway and the Near-Death Experience." *Journal of Medical Humanities* 20 (1999) 203–17. https:// dx.doi.org/10.1023/A:1022982413557.

Vincent, Milly. "Incredible Moment Teenager, 18, Who Was Declared Brain-dead Blinks and Starts Breathing on His Own Just as His Parents Were Poised to Turn Off His Life Support and Donate His Organs." *Daily Mail* (2021).

Voss, Robert S., Kristofer M. Helgen and Sharon A. Jansa. "Extraordinary Claims Require Extraordinary Evidence: A Comment on Cozzuol et al. (2013)." *Journal of Mammalogy* 95.4 (2014) 893–98.

Wainwright, William J. *Mysticism: A Study of Its Nature, Cognitive Value, and Moral Implications*. Madison: University of Wisconsin Press, 1981.

Zaleski, Carol. *Otherworld Journeys: Accounts of near-Death Experience in Medieval and Modern Times*. New York: Oxford University Press, 1988.

Index

INDEX

Distortion of time, 3, 7
Dossey, Larry, 15
Dreams, 7, 8, 24–26, 29
Dreier, Jens P., 24–25, 30
Drugs, 4, 8, 50, 56, 57, 58

Er, 16
Evidence, x, 1, 2, 3, 12, 39, 40, 41,
    43, 44, 46, 47, 49, 50, 51,
    53, 54, 63, 64, 65, 68, 69,
    72, 74, 77, 78, 80
Extraordinary, 44, 46, 50, 51, 69
Evangelize, 70
Evangelism, 69, 70, 77
Eyewitness, 42, 49, 75–77, 78, 80

False memories, 30, 33, 34, 58, 72
Family members, xii, 46, 49, 53, 79
Fantasy, 30–33, 58
Fischer, John, 7–8
Flew, Anthony, 18, 19, 45–46

Geisler, Norman, 44–45, 67–68
Greene, H. Leon, 60–63, 72–74, 80
Greyson, Bruce, 9–12, 22
Groothuis, Douglas, 2, 54, 69, 73
Guide, 16, 47

Habermas, Gary, xii, 2, 5, 8–9,
    10, 18, 19, 38–46, 46–50,
    52–65, 67–79
Hallucinations, 8, 20, 25, 26, 29,
    30, 58
Hebrews 9:27, 13, 56
Heaven, 1, 12–13, 16, 17, 18, 36,
    38, 49, 57, 71
    Tourism, 12–13
Heaven Is for Real, 12–13
Hell, 56, 57
Holden, Janice Minor, 24–25
Hume, David, 40–41, 43–46
    Humean, 44–45, 78
Hypothermia, 4

Jesus, xii, 1, 37, 39, 42, 55, 60–61,
    71, 73, 77–79, 82

Kondziella, Daniel, 26–30, 72

Lazarus, 37
Levitan, Harold, 26
Life support, 4, 5, 14
Light, 3, 6, 9, 16, 17, 29, 46, 48, 53,
    55, 57, 70, 71, 74, 80
Lizza, John, 4–5
Long, Jeffrey, 5–7, 24–25
Long haul response, 11

Malarkey, Alex, 13
Martial, Charlotte, 6–7, 30–36, 46,
    58, 72
Mental illness, 33
Medicine, 12, 15
Memory, 15, 21, 30, 33–35, 56, 58,
    72, 74, 75
    Distorted, 34, 75
    False, 30–31, 33–35, 58, 72
Migraine, 26–29, 72
Miles, Steven, 4–5
Miracle, x, 41–45, 77–78
    Fatima, 42–43, 77
    Miracles from Heaven, 13
Mitchell-Yellin, Benjamin, 7–8
Moody, Raymond, 6, 8
Moral argument, 73
Moreland, J. P., 47–50, 54–65, 68,
    72–73
Morse, Melvin, 47–50, 53, 57–58,
    62, 76
Mortality, ix, 1, 18, 82

Naturalism, 1, 2, 52, 63, 66, 68, 69,
    70, 80, 82
Naturalist, xii, 1, 2, 18, 37, 38, 39,
    40, 41, 45, 57, 60, 68, 70,
    74, 78, 79, 81
Near-death experience
    Classical, 10, 32

Index

Hellish, 9, 10, 19, 56, 57
Inverse, 9–10, 56
Void, 10
New outlook, 8

Olsen, Mark Harboe, 23, 25
Out-of-body experience, 6, 7, 16,
    27, 36, 46, 48, 52, 53, 59,
    62, 73, 74, 76

Paul, the Apostle, 42, 61, 79
Perry, Paul, 47
Personhood, 4
Plato, 16
Presuppositionalism, 68
Purgatory, 5

Rawlings, Maurice, 49–50, 56
Research, 7, 10, 14, 19–24, 26,
    28–30, 32–33, 36, 37, 39,
    46, 50, 53, 56, 58, 59, 62,
    63, 71, 76, 77
Researchers, 53, 65, 76
Resurrection, xii, 13, 39, 43, 44, 61,
    77–79, 82
Resuscitation, 8, 14, 15, 20, 21,
    48–50, 56, 75

Sagan, Carl, 40, 46, 50
Scientific method, 1, 61–62
Shapiro, Ben, 73
Sharp, Kimberly Clark, 65, 76, 77
Skeptic, 9, 18, 42, 81
Skepticism, 40, 78
Skeptical, 8, 40, 45, 62
Sleep, 22–27, 29, 50
    REM, 23–27, 29
Steelman, 73–74
Straw man, 72–73
Supernatural, xi, 8, 16, 18, 40, 46,
    59, 60, 62, 64, 66, 70, 74

The Boy Who Came Back From
    Heaven, 13
The Republic, 16
Theists, 18, 37, 73, 77
Trauma, 11, 22–23, 34
Tunnel, 6, 9, 16, 48, 53

Wainwright, William, 55
Westbrook, Thomas, 77
Word association, 33
Worldviews, 1, 2, 38, 54–55, 60, 68

www.ingramcontent.com/pod-product-compliance
Lightning Source LLC
Chambersburg PA
CBHW062344300326
41947CB00012B/1207